Reading 4

with answers

Liz Driscoll

CAMBRIDGE
UNIVERSITY PRESS

CAMBRIDGE UNIVERSITY PRESS
Cambridge, New York, Melbourne, Madrid, Cape Town, Singapore, São Paulo, Delhi

Cambridge University Press
The Edinburgh Building, Cambridge CB2 8RU, UK

www.cambridge.org
Information on this title: www.cambridge.org/9780521705752

First published 2008

Printed in the United Kingdom at the University Press, Cambridge

A catalogue record for this publication is available from the British Library

ISBN-13 978-0-521-70575-2

Contents

Map of the book

Unit number	Title	Topic	How to ...
Social and Travel			
1	**I'll take it!**	Shopping	<ul><li>scan a text for specific words and information</li><li>understand what a guarantee covers</li><li>follow a recommendation and choose a film to watch</li></ul>
2	**Take care of yourself**	Health	<ul><li>skim a text from a guidebook in order to get a general impression</li><li>appreciate health risks and the precautions which you need to take</li><li>follow instructions and carry out exercises</li></ul>
3	**Our flight's delayed**	Travel	<ul><li>work out the meaning of words from their context – and from other similar words you know</li><li>find out flight details from a ticket and rearranged details from a letter</li><li>understand an insurance policy and consider whether to make a claim</li></ul>
4	**I've been burgled**	Dealing with an emergency	<ul><li>understand a letter from the police</li><li>interpret punctuation and use it to read a text efficiently</li><li>separate information and advice, and follow advice about protecting your home</li></ul>
5	**Picasso's birthplace**	Tourism	<ul><li>infer meaning when it is not stated directly</li><li>find out about a museum and decide whether or not to visit it</li><li>follow a route</li></ul>
6	**Love it or loathe it!**	Newspaper articles	<ul><li>relate the contents of an article to its title</li><li>recognize rhetorical questions</li><li>read authentic newspaper articles and extract the main points</li><li>distinguish between opinions and facts</li></ul>
Work and Study			
7	**Import, export!**	Business correspondence	<ul><li>understand general business correspondence</li><li>identify new terms in a text and ask for clarification</li><li>identify the purpose of an email in a business context</li></ul>
8	**I've got an interview**	Recruitment and interview	<ul><li>relate your own experiences to what you read in a text</li><li>read an interview guidance pack and prepare for an interview</li><li>understand questions you will be asked and the reasoning behind them</li></ul>

Unit number	Title	Topic	How to ...
9	**What's your new job like?**	Terms and conditions	o rephrase formal language into more neutral everyday language o understand part of a legal contract about annual holidays o understand a letter about pay cycles
10	**I've got Thursday off**	Flexitime	o understand the benefits of working flexitime o understand a description of a system which monitors staff attendance o identify the most important noun in a group of nouns
11	**I've read the minutes**	Minutes and reports	o understand the minutes of a meeting and act upon them o use headings to predict the content of a report o understand a report and consider its implications
12	**The course is in English**	Choosing a university course	o interpret signalling words and phrases, and use them to understand a text o evaluate reasons for choosing a university overseas o understand a homepage about universities in Australia
13	**Read faster!**	Increasing your reading speed	o appreciate the benefits of reading faster o overcome obstacles to faster reading o practise reading faster
14	**I've chosen this topic**	Using a reference book	o skim the back cover in order to assess the suitability of a book for your studies o scan the Contents and Index, and find the entries within the book o assess the suitability of text extracts for your purposes o make notes on the main points of text extracts
15	**English today**	How English is used today	o identify how a paragraph is organized o use your knowledge of paragraph organization to help you understand a text o distinguish between the main points of a paragraph/text and examples
16	**I need a good score**	Sampling the IELTS exam	o follow exam tips and put them into practice o understand paraphrases o carry out exam tasks

Work and Study

Acknowledgements

I would particularly like to thank Caroline Thiriau, of Cambridge University Press, for her support and guidance in the writing of both this book and the other *Real Reading* books in the series. I am also grateful to Nóirín Burke, who commissioned the project, Sue F Jones for her involvement in the editing and Linda Matthews for overseeing the production of this book. My thanks also go to Stephanie White and Paul Fellows for their wonderful design work.

I am extremely grateful to my friend and former student Margret Rappel, without whose involvement Unit 7 would not exist. My thanks also go to Valerie Barnish, Barbara Dennis, Ian Lees and Maria-José Luque Arribal for their help in finding some of the other texts.

The author and publishers are grateful to the following reviewers for their valuable insights and suggestions:

Steve Banfield, UAE; Ildiko Berke, Hungary; Ian Chisholm, UK; Alper Darici, Turkey; Rosie Ganne, UK; Elif Isler, Turkey; Kathy Kolarik, Australia; Veni Krishnaveni, Malaysia; Jessica Mackay, Spain; Steve Miller, UK; Ersoy Osman, UK; Wayne Trotman, Turkey

The authors and publishers acknowledge the following sources of copyright material and are grateful for the permissions granted. While every effort has been made, it has not always been possible to identify the sources of all the material used, or to trace all copyright holders. If any omissions are brought to our notice, we will be happy to include the appropriate acknowledgements on reprinting.

pp. 10–11: adapted 'Receipt and Guarantee'. Used by permission of DSG International PLC; p. 12: DVD cover text 'The Shawshank Redemption' Copyright © 1994 Castle Rock Entertainment; pp. 14–15: text 'Health' from *The Rough Guide to New Zealand* (Rough Guides 2004). Copyright © Laura Harper, Tony Mudd and Paul Whitfield, 2004, pp. 68–71: text from *The English Language* by David Crystal (Penguin Books 1998). Copyright © David Crystal, 1998, pp. 80–81: text from *Port Out, Starboard Home* by Michael Quinion (Penguin Books 2004, 2005). Copyright © Michael Quinion, 2004. Reproduced by permission of Penguin Books Ltd; p. 16: text 'Deep Vein Thrombosis (DVT)'. Reproduced by permission of Sanofi Pasteur MSD; p. 17: text 'Your Inflight Exercises' from *High Life Magazine*. Used by permission of British Airways and Body Control Pilates Group; p. 18: 'BA E-ticket', p.19: 'BA Letter'. Reproduced by kind permission of British Airways; pp. 20–21: 'AllClear Travel Insurance Policy'. Reproduced by permission of BAS Insurance Services; p. 23: adapted 'Thames Valley Police Letter'. Copyright © Thames Valley Police, Crime Investigation Management Unit, Oxfordshire Basic Command Unit. Used by Permission of Thames Valley Police; pp. 24–25: text 'Beat the Burglar'. Crown Copyright © 2007; pp. 26–27: Leaflet '2016 Málaga' from *MLG Málaga en tus Manos*. Edited by Malaka. Clack. SL. Used by kind permission of Málaga en tus Manos; pp. 28–29: text 'Picasso's return' by José Antonio del Cañizo and map from the leaflet *Málaga Park and its surrounding Monuments*. Used by permission of Fundación Málaga; p. 30: 'Sudoku Puzzle' from *Times Sudoku Book 1*, by Times Books. Reprinted by permission of HarperCollins Publishers Ltd. Copyright © Times Books, 2005; p. 31: text 'The World Beater' by Richard Morrison. Times Online, 30 June 2006. Copyright © NI Syndication Limited 2006; p. 32: text 'Sudoku Mind Games' by Robert Lipsyte, *USA Today*, 6 October 2006. Copyright © Robert Lipsyte, used by permission of Robert Lipsyte. www.robertlipsyte.com; p. 34: text 'Bites and Stings' from *Holiday Health Leaflet*. Copyright © Alliance UniChem 2005; pp. 41–42: text from Hays Office Support Brochure. Content supplied with the kind permission of Hays Specialist Recruitment. Hays plc is a FTSE 250 company and the largest specialist recruitment agency in the UK. Visit hays.com to search for vacancies, view candidate profiles and to find your nearest office; pp. 49–51: text 'Flexitime' and 'ATRACS Web Enabled Attendance Management' from www.borer.co.uk. Used by permission of Borer Data Systems Limited; pp. 56–57: text 'Pre-departure decisions' and p. 77: text 'Tutorials' from *Study Skills for Speakers of English as a Second Language*. Copyright © Marilyn Lewis and Hayo Reinders 2003, pp. 64–67: text from *Contemporary America, revised 2nd edition*. Copyright © Russell Duncan and Joseph Goddard 2003, 2005. Reproduced with permission of Palgrave Macmillan; pp. 58–59: text 'Why study Oz?' from the website www.InternationalStudent.com. Copyright © InternationalStudent.com; pp. 60–63: text from *Practical Faster Reading*. Copyright © 1976 G Mosback and V Mosback, pp. 72–73: 'Summary completion' from *Action Plan for IELTS*. Copyright © 2006 Vanessa Jakeman and Clare McDowell. *Action Plan for IELTS* is a last-minute revision guide for IELTS candidates, pp. 74–75: 'Soft Centres – hard profits' from *Insight into IELTS Extra*. Copyright © 2003 Vanessa Jakeman and Clare McDowell. *Insight into IELTS* is a skills-based IELTS course book, pp. 92–95: Dictionary entries from *Cambridge Advanced Learner's Dictionary, 2nd edition*, 2005. Reproduced by permission of Cambridge University Press; p. 76: text 'How strictly is IELTS marked?' from IELTS leaflet: Information for Candidates. Reproduced by permission of University of Cambridge ESOL Examinations; pp.77: text 'Food retail' from The Midcounties Interim Report for the 16 weeks ended 29 July 2006, p. 78: text 'Absence from Work' from Midcounties Co-operative Staff Handbook. Reproduced by permission of The Midcounties Co-operative Limited.

The authors and publishers would like to thank the following for permission to reproduce photographs:

Key: l = left, c = centre, r = right, t = top, b = bottom

Alamy/©Popperfoto for p. 26, /©Andrea Matone for p. 52; Getty Images/©Stone for p14; Rex for p. 12 (b); The Kobal Collection/ ©Castle Rock Entertainment for p. 12 (t); p. 74: Paul Mulcahy for the photo 'box of soft centre chocolates' Copyright © Paul Mulcahy.

Illustrations:

Mark Duffin p. 36; Kamae Design p. 29

Text design and page make-up: Kamae Design, Oxford
Cover design: Kamae Design, Oxford
Cover photo: Getty
Picture research: Hilary Luckcock

Introduction
To the student

Who is *Real Reading 4* for?

You can use this book if you are a student at advanced level and you want to improve your English reading. You can use the book alone without a teacher or you can use it in a classroom with a teacher.

How will *Real Reading 4* help me with my reading?

Real Reading 4 contains texts for everyday reading practice, for example leaflets, notices, websites, newspapers, etc. It is designed to help you with reading you will need to do in English at home or when visiting another country.

The exercises in each unit help you develop useful skills such as working out the meaning of unknown words from context and ignoring parts of the text which are not useful to you. *Real Reading 4* discourages you from using a dictionary to find out the meaning of every word you don't know.

How is *Real Reading 4* organized?

The book has 16 units and is divided into two sections:
- Units 1–6 – social and travel situations
- Units 7–16 – work and study situations

Every unit is divided into Reading A and Reading B and has:
- *Get ready to read*: to introduce you to the topic of the unit
- *Learning tip*: to help you improve your learning
- *Class bonus*: an exercise you can do with other students or friends
- *Focus on*: to help you study useful grammar or vocabulary
- *Did you know?*: extra information about vocabulary, different cultures or the topic of the unit
- *Extra practice*: an extra exercise for more practice
- *Can-do checklist*: to help you think about what you learnt in the unit

After each section there is a review unit. The reviews help you practise the skills you learn in each section.

At the back of the book you can find:
- *Appendices*: contain lists of *Useful language*, *Learning tips* for every unit and information about *Using a dictionary*
- *Answer key*: gives correct answers and possible answers for exercises that have more than one answer

How can I use *Real Reading 4*?

The units at the end of the book are more difficult than the units at the beginning of the book. However, you do not need to do the units in order. It is better to choose the units that are most interesting for you and to do them in the order you prefer.

There are many different ways you can use this book. We suggest you work in this way:
- Look in the *Contents* list and find a unit that interests you.
- Prepare yourself for reading by working through the *Get ready to read* exercises.
- Look at *Appendix 1: Useful language* for the unit.
- Do the exercises in Reading A. Use the example answers to guide you. Put the *Learning tip* into practice (either in Reading A or Reading B).
- Do the exercises in Reading B.
- Check your answers with your teacher or with the *Answer key*.
- If you want to do more work, do the *Extra practice* activity.
- At the end of the unit, think about what you have learnt and complete the *Can-do checklist*.
- Look at the list of *Learning tips* in *Appendix 2* and decide which other tips you have used in the unit.

Introduction
To the teacher

What is *Cambridge English Skills*?

Real Reading 4 is one of 12 books in the *Cambridge English Skills* series. The series also contains *Real Writing* and *Real Listening & Speaking* books and offers skills training to students from elementary to advanced level. All the books are available in with-answers and without-answers editions.

Level	Book	Author
Elementary CEF: A2 Cambridge ESOL: KET NQF Skills for life: Entry 2	Real Reading 1 with answers	Liz Driscoll
	Real Reading 1 without answers	Liz Driscoll
	Real Writing 1 with answers and audio CD	Graham Palmer
	Real Writing 1 without answers	Graham Palmer
	Real Listening & Speaking 1 with answers and audio CDs (2)	Miles Craven
	Real Listening & Speaking 1 without answers	Miles Craven
Pre-intermediate CEF: B1 Cambridge ESOL: PET NQF Skills for life: Entry 3	Real Reading 2 with answers	Liz Driscoll
	Real Reading 2 without answers	Liz Driscoll
	Real Writing 2 with answers and audio CD	Graham Palmer
	Real Writing 2 without answers	Graham Palmer
	Real Listening & Speaking 2 with answers and audio CDs (2)	Sally Logan & Craig Thaine
	Real Listening & Speaking 2 without answers	Sally Logan & Craig Thaine
Intermediate to upper-intermediate CEF: B2 Cambridge ESOL: FCE NQF Skills for life: Level 1	Real Reading 3 with answers	Liz Driscoll
	Real Reading 3 without answers	Liz Driscoll
	Real Writing 3 with answers and audio CD	Roger Gower
	Real Writing 3 without answers	Roger Gower
	Real Listening & Speaking 3 with answers and audio CDs (2)	Miles Craven
	Real Listening & Speaking 3 without answers	Miles Craven
Advanced CEF: C1 Cambridge ESOL: CAE NQF Skills for life: Level 2	Real Reading 4 with answers	Liz Driscoll
	Real Reading 4 without answers	Liz Driscoll
	Real Writing 4 with answers and audio CD	Simon Haines
	Real Writing 4 without answers	Simon Haines
	Real Listening & Speaking 4 with answers and audio CDs (2)	Miles Craven
	Real Listening & Speaking 4 without answers	Miles Craven

Where are the teacher's notes?

The series is accompanied by a dedicated website containing detailed teaching notes and extension ideas for every unit of every book. Please visit www.cambridge.org/englishskills to access the *Cambridge English Skills* teacher's notes.

What are the main aims of *Real Reading 4*?

- To help students develop reading skills in accordance with the ALTE (Association of Language Testers in Europe) Can-do statements. These statements describe what language users can typically do at different levels and in different contexts. Visit www.alte.org for further information.
- To encourage autonomous learning by focusing on learner training.

What are the key features of *Real Reading 4*?

- *Real Reading 4* is aimed at advanced learners of English at level C1 of the Council of Europe's CEFR (Common European Framework of Reference for Languages).
- The book contains 16 four-page units, divided into two sections: *Social and Travel*, and *Work and Study*.
- *Real Reading 4* units are divided into Reading A and Reading B and contain:
  - *Get ready to read* warm-up exercises to get students thinking about the topic
  - *Learning tips* which give students advice on how to improve their reading and their learning
  - *Class bonus* communication activities for pairwork and group work so that you can adapt the material to suit your classes
  - *Focus on* exercises which provide contextualized practice in particular grammar or vocabulary areas
  - *Did you know?* boxes which provide notes on cultural or linguistic differences between English-speaking countries, or factual information on the topic of the unit
  - *Extra practice* extension tasks which provide more real world reading practice
  - *Can-do checklists* at the end of every unit to encourage students to think about what they have learnt
- There are two review units to practise skills that have been introduced in the units.
- It has an international feel and contains a range of texts from English-speaking – and other – countries.
- It can be used as self-study material, in class, or as supplementary homework material.

What is the best way to use *Real Reading 4* in the classroom?

The book is designed so that the units may be used in any order, although the more difficult units naturally appear near the end of the book, in the *Work and Study* section.

You can consult the unit-by-unit teacher's notes at www.cambridge.org/englishskills for detailed teaching ideas. However, broadly speaking, different parts of the book can be approached in the following ways:

- *Useful language*: You can use the *Useful language* lists in *Appendix 1* to preteach or revise the vocabulary from the unit you are working on.
- *Get ready to read*: It is a good idea to use this section as an introduction to the topic. Students can work on the exercises in pairs or groups. Many of these require students to answer questions about their personal experience. These questions can be used as prompts for discussion. Some exercises contain a problem-solving element that students can work on together. Other exercises aim to clarify key vocabulary in the unit. You can present these vocabulary items directly to students.
- *Learning tips*: You can ask students to read and discuss these in an open-class situation. An alternative approach is for you to create a series of discussion questions associated with the *Learning tip*. Students can discuss their ideas in pairs or small groups followed by open-class feedback. The *Learning tip* acts as a reflective learning tool to help promote learner autonomy.
- *Class bonuses*: The material in these activities aims to provide freer practice. You can set these up carefully, then take the role of observer during the activity so that students carry out the task freely. You can make yourself available to help students or analyze the language they produce during the activity.
- *Extra practice*: These can be set as homework or out-of-class projects for your students. Alternatively, students can do some activities in pairs during class time.
- *Can-do checklists*: Refer to these at the beginning of a lesson to explain to students what the lesson will cover, and again at the end so that students can evaluate their learning for themselves.
- *Appendices*: You may find it useful to refer your students to the *Useful language*, *Learning tips* and *Using a dictionary* sections. Students can use these as general checklists to help them with their reading.

Unit 1
I'll take it!

go to Useful language p. 82

Get ready to read

- A customer is returning an MP3 player to the store where he bought it. Who says these things – the customer (C) or the shop assistant (S)? (Make sure you understand the meaning of the words in *italics*.)
  a Have you got the *receipt*? ☐
  b I've checked, and it's still under *guarantee*. ☐
  c I'd like to *exchange* it for another one. ☐
  d You can have a *refund* for the full amount. ☐

- Underline the words in these sentences so that they are true for you.
  I like / I don't like watching movies.
  I sometimes / never go to the cinema.
  I like / I don't like watching films on TV.
  I sometimes / never rent DVDs.
  I've got / I haven't got a collection of DVDs.
  I sometimes / never watch films in their original version.

A Contact your personal adviser

1 Roberto has been to an electrical store and bought a DVD player. Look at the receipt and answer these questions.

   a When did he buy the DVD player? _____
   b How much did it cost? _____
   c What should he do with the receipt? Why? _____

Branch: 240 OXFORD MK/PL

Till: 2   Receipt: 024530   Date: 24/09/20_

Operator: 31 KARIM   Time: 10:54

```
THANK YOU FOR YOUR CUSTOM
FOR FURTHER ASSISTANCE PLEASE
CONTACT YOUR PERSONAL ADVISOR:
            KARIM
         Assistant 31
        On 08706087182
```

SALE

Assistant 31 KARIM

SAMSUNG DVD-1080P7 DVD PLAYER   £69.99
1 x 0000868202 @ £69.99

AMOUNT DUE   £69.99

TOTAL TENDERED   £69.99

PLEASE KEEP YOUR RECEIPT. IT MAY BE
REQUIRED FOR REFUNDS OR EXCHANGES

Learning tip

We use a technique called scanning when we search a text for a particular word or words. This involves looking quickly at the text without considering the meaning. Once we have found what we are looking for, we may then read the text around the word(s).

2 Look at the leaflet on the opposite page. Roberto got this leaflet when he bought the DVD player. Underline the words *exchange* and *refund* as quickly as you can. (Note: both words appear more than once!)

3 Now read the first section and answer these questions.

   a Under what circumstances could Roberto get an exchange or a refund? _____
   b Is there a time limit? _____
   c In what condition would he have to return the DVD player to the shop? (Note: Roberto didn't get any gifts or accessories with the DVD player.)
   _____

4 Now read the second section and answer these questions.

   a Under what other circumstances could Roberto get an exchange or a refund?
   _____
   b What is the time limit for getting an exchange or a refund?
   _____
   c In what condition would he have to return the DVD player to the shop? _____

Thank you for shopping with us

1 **Changed your mind?**

If you bought your product in one of our stores and have now changed your mind, we will exchange or refund it within seven days of purchase. This does not apply if the item was specially ordered for you or was a fully guaranteed exchanged product.
The product must be:
- Unopened (with any seal intact)
- Unused
- Returned complete with any free gifts you received with the product.

Contact your local store with your receipt details to arrange your refund or exchange.

2 **Your Guarantee**

The following are guidelines. We treat each case on its individual circumstances.
- We will always offer you the choice of an exchange or refund if your product develops a fault within 28 days of delivery.
- To receive a refund, the product must be in otherwise "as new" condition complete with all accessories and free gifts supplied with it. If possible, please return the product in its original packaging.
- If your product develops a fault within 12 months of purchase, we will offer a prompt repair service.
- To obtain a repair for your product, call the relevant helpline number on the back page of this leaflet. If your product is not listed, return it to your local store.
- This guarantee does not cover faults caused through accident, neglect, misuse or normal wear and tear.
- Faulty software, pre-recorded video tapes, DVDs, Minidiscs and CDs will be exchanged for the same title or refunded.

3 **Our Price Promise**

In the unlikely event that you find a cheaper identical product or offer immediately available from another retail store within 10 miles of your local store we will not only match their price but also give you an extra 10% of the difference. Our Price Promise also applies for up to 7 days after you make your purchase with us; just bring your receipt to claim your refund. This Price Promise does not apply to clearance or ex-display products, special orders, closing down sales, members only, extended warranty prices, Internet or telephone order line purchases.

Focus on ...
the negative prefix
un- with past participles

1 The prefix *un-* means 'not' as in the verbs *undo*, *undress*, *unload*. *Un-* can also be added to a past participle to make a negative adjective, e.g. *unexpected*, *unfinished*, *unknown*. Underline two examples of *un-* + past participle in the first section of the leaflet.

2 Complete these sentences with *un-* + the past participles of the verbs in the box.

> aid   ~~answer~~   commit   cut   employ   speak

a Questions from local residents remained
   ..*unanswered*... .
b Since his accident, he hasn't been able to walk
   ....
c He's been .... for over a year.
d Five senators have admitted they are still
   .... on the taxation question.
e There's an .... assumption in the department that Sue will take over the post when Ian leaves.
f We saw the original, ... version of the film.

5 Now read the third section and answer these questions.

a Why does this section mention *refund* – but not *exchange*?
----
b Under what circumstances could Roberto get a refund?
----
c Is there a time limit?
----

6 How much refund – if any – would Roberto get if he saw the same DVD player for £59.99 in the following situations?

a in another shop in Oxford on September 26th
----
b in another shop in Oxford on October 10th
----
c in a shop in London (90 kilometres / 60 miles from Oxford)
----
d on the Internet on September 26th
----

7 Do you always keep receipts? Have you ever needed one?

B It's a great movie!

1 Roberto wants to buy a DVD to watch on his new DVD player. His friend Ivan has told him about a couple of films. Read what Ivan says in a and b on the right. Do you recognize these films? What are they called?

2 Roberto has found one of the films that Ivan mentioned. Look at the back of the DVD case quickly. Match the film with one of the descriptions in Exercise 1.

Did you know …?

Academy Awards are annual cinema prizes. They have been awarded since 1927 by the American Academy of Motion Pictures. An Academy Award is often referred to as an 'Oscar'. The origin of this nickname is unknown, although one theory suggests that academy librarian and eventual executive director, Margaret Herrick, said that the small statue looked like her Uncle Oscar. The name was well enough known for Walt Disney to use in his 1934 acceptance speech.

3 Underline the information on the back of the DVD case which gives the answers to these questions.

a What happened to the main character before he went to jail?

b What happens to the main character while he is in jail?

a This film is set in a prison in the 1930s, I think. The main character is a prison guard, and the film is about the relationship he has with one of the prisoners. This man has committed an awful crime and he's on death row, but he's really a gentle giant. He's even afraid of the dark!

b It's about two men who meet in jail. The older one has been there for years. The other one, who's the main character, never expected to end up in jail. The men are from very different backgrounds, but they become great friends. They help each other and learn a lot from each other. And I don't want to tell you the ending!

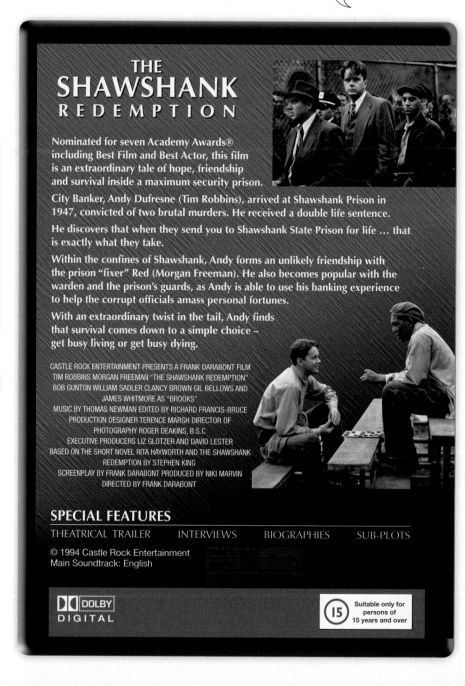

THE
SHAWSHANK
R E D E M P T I O N

Nominated for seven Academy Awards® including Best Film and Best Actor, this film is an extraordinary tale of hope, friendship and survival inside a maximum security prison.

City Banker, Andy Dufresne (Tim Robbins), arrived at Shawshank Prison in 1947, convicted of two brutal murders. He received a double life sentence.

He discovers that when they send you to Shawshank State Prison for life … that is exactly what they take.

Within the confines of Shawshank, Andy forms an unlikely friendship with the prison "fixer" Red (Morgan Freeman). He also becomes popular with the warden and the prison's guards, as Andy is able to use his banking experience to help the corrupt officials amass personal fortunes.

With an extraordinary twist in the tail, Andy finds that survival comes down to a simple choice – get busy living or get busy dying.

CASTLE ROCK ENTERTAINMENT PRESENTS A FRANK DARABONT FILM TIM ROBBINS MORGAN FREEMAN "THE SHAWSHANK REDEMPTION" BOB GUNTON WILLIAM SADLER CLANCY BROWN GIL BELLOWS AND JAMES WHITMORE AS "BROOKS" MUSIC BY THOMAS NEWMAN EDITED BY RICHARD FRANCIS-BRUCE PRODUCTION DESIGNER TERENCE MARSH DIRECTOR OF PHOTOGRAPHY ROGER DEAKINS, B.S.C EXECUTIVE PRODUCERS LIZ GLOTZER AND DAVID LESTER BASED ON THE SHORT NOVEL RITA HAYWORTH AND THE SHAWSHANK REDEMPTION BY STEPHEN KING SCREENPLAY BY FRANK DARABONT PRODUCED BY NIKI MARVIN DIRECTED BY FRANK DARABONT

SPECIAL FEATURES

THEATRICAL TRAILER   INTERVIEWS   BIOGRAPHIES   SUB-PLOTS

© 1994 Castle Rock Entertainment
Main Soundtrack: English

DOLBY DIGITAL

(15) Suitable only for persons of 15 years and over

4 Here are some other things that Ivan says about *The Shawshank Redemption*. Read each statement and scan the back of the DVD case quickly and find out if he was right or wrong. Put a tick ✓ or a cross ✗ and note any further information the DVD case gives you.

a | It's quite an old film – it was released in the early 1990s, I think. | ☐

b | It's quite long – more than two hours, I think. | ☐

c | I seem to remember that one of the actors got an Oscar nomination. | ☐

d | The director isn't very famous – I've never heard of him. | ☐

e | I'm not sure, but I think Tom Hanks played one of the characters. | ☐

f | It's based on a book by someone famous. | ☐

5 The title *The Shawshank Redemption* refers to what happens in the film. *Redemption* means 'when someone is saved from evil, suffering, etc.'. Who do you think is likely to be saved?

6 If you haven't already seen *The Shawshank Redemption*, would you be interested in seeing it? Why? / Why not?

7 Read this review from the Internet. Does this influence your decision about seeing the film?

http://www.dvdreviews.com/theshawshankredemption

THE SHAWSHANK REDEMPTION

★★★★★ **The best movie ever made**
by priya 42174

127 of **143** people found this review helpful

When I first started watching this movie, I was like, oh great, another slow movie about prison life. Somewhere along the way, I forgot I was watching a movie. I became so engrossed in it that I felt like I was in the film, and part of it.
The movie is absolutely riveting, the narration is incredible, and the story … wow, what a story! Put that together with a great cast and one of the best endings of all time, and you have a timeless classic.

E✗tra practice

Find other reviews of *The Shawshank Redemption* on the Internet. Alternatively, watch the film in English.

Class bonus

Choose a film you have enjoyed. Write a short review. Create a review noticeboard in the classroom. Will you follow any of your friends' recommendations?

Can-do checklist

Tick what you can do.

	Can do	Need more practice
I can scan a text for specific words and information.		
I can understand what a guarantee covers.		
I can follow a recommendation and choose a film to watch.		

Unit2
Take care of yourself

Get ready to read

- What things do you read in connection with your holiday before you go away? Tick ✓ the boxes.
  holiday brochures ☐
  a guidebook ☐
  websites ☐

- Answer these questions. Write *Y* (yes) or *N* (no) in the boxes.
  Have you ever been bitten by an insect? ☐
  Have you ever been caught in an earthquake? ☐
  Have you ever had too much sun? ☐
  Have you ever fallen off a motorbike? ☐
  Have you ever been bitten by a dog? ☐
  Have you ever eaten something that's made you sick? ☐

- Have any of the things above happened to you on holiday?

go to Useful language p. 83

A What are the health issues?

1 You are planning a trip to New Zealand and your English teacher has lent you a guidebook. Read the introduction on the right to the *Health* section from the guidebook. Are travellers likely to have medical problems when they visit New Zealand?

 **Health**

B
BASICS | Health

New Zealand is relatively free of serious health hazards and the most common pitfalls are not taking precautions or simply underestimating the power of nature. No vaccinations are required to enter the country, but you should make sure you have adequate cover in your health insurance, especially if you plan to take on the Great Outdoors.

Did you know …?

A creature you are unlikely to see in New Zealand is the kiwi. The kiwi is New Zealand's national symbol. It is a flightless bird, dull brown in colour and very, very shy. There are fewer than 15,000 birds in the country (they are not found anywhere else in the world) and the kiwi may soon become extinct in the wild. *Kiwi* is also an informal word for a person from New Zealand.

Learning tip

When we read a text for the first time, we often use a technique known as *skimming* – looking over a text rapidly to get a general impression. This does not remove the need for careful reading later, but it allows us to select parts of the text that are worth re-reading. We then read these particular phrases, sentences or sections more carefully in order to understand the details. Remember that there are different ways in which we can read a text, and the technique we use depends on the type of text and our reason for reading.

2 **Skim the rest of the *Health* section. Do these paragraphs change your answer to the question in Exercise 1 in any way?**

3 **Read paragraphs 2–5 again. Choose words from the text (1–3 words from each paragraph) which can act as paragraph headings.**

Focus on ...
colloquial language

Colloquial language is informal language which is often used in speech rather than writing. The guidebook extract in Exercise 2 contains several examples of colloquial language because it is written in a conversational style.

1 Find colloquial words in the text which are used instead of the following:
   a large (paragraph 1)
   ....hefty............
   b alcoholic drinks (paragraph 2)
   ....
   c put on (paragraph 3)
   ....
   d nasty creatures (paragraph 4)
   ....
   e creature (paragraph 4)
   ....
   f annoying creatures (paragraph 5)
   ....

2 The words in *italics* are all examples of colloquial language. What is the neutral equivalent?
   a I'm going to have a *kip*. I'm really exhausted. ......sleep......
   b My sister's already got four *kids*, and now she's expecting another!
   ....
   c The tickets to London cost 20 *quid* each. ....
   d I can't pay my rent this month. *I'm broke.* ....
   e Jorge will know the answer. He's really *brainy*.
   ....
   f I've known Sajid for ages. He's a good *mate* of mine.
   ....

1 New Zealand has a fine health service, despite recent government cuts, and medical services are reasonably cheap by world standards. Although all visitors are covered by the accident compensation scheme, under which you can claim some medical and hospital expenses, in the event of an accident without full accident cover in your travel insurance, you could still face a hefty bill. For more minor ailments, you can visit a doctor for a consultation (around $35) and, armed with a prescription, buy any required medication at a pharmacy at a reasonable price.

2 Perhaps the most hazardous element of the whole New Zealand experience is getting there, in the light of a growing realization that long periods of time spent in cramped conditions on aeroplanes can contribute to deep vein thrombosis (DVT). All the airlines now have videos telling you to move about, perform stationary callisthenics and drink plenty of water. It also helps to limit the amount of booze you consume and, if you are unsure, contact your GP before travelling to find out if you are predisposed towards this problem and what you can do about it.

3 Visitors to New Zealand frequently get caught out by the intensity of the sun, its damaging ultra-violet rays easily penetrating the thin ozone layer and reducing burn times to as little as ten minutes in spring and summer. Stay out of the sun as much as possible between 11am and 3pm, and always slap on plenty of sunblock. Reapply every few hours as well as after swimming, and keep a check on any moles on your body: if you notice any changes, during or after a trip, see your doctor straight away.

4 New Zealand's wildlife is amazingly benign. There are no snakes, scorpions and other nasties, and there's only one poisonous creature: the little katipo spider. Mercifully rare, this six-millimetre-long critter (the biting female is black with a red patch) is found in coastal areas and only bites if disturbed. The bite can be fatal, but antivenin is available in most hospitals, is effective up to three days after a bite and no one has died from an encounter with the spider for many years.

5 A far bigger problem are mosquitoes and sandflies which are a great irritant, but generally free of life-threatening diseases. The West Coast of the South Island in the summer is the worst place for these beasts, though they appear to a lesser degree in many other places across the country: a liberal application of repellent keeps them at bay.

4 **What precautions are recommended for the hazards? Make notes in the chart. (Note: no precautions are suggested for one hazard.)**

paragraph	hazard	precautions	remedies
2	DVT	move about in the plane	
3			
4			
5			

5 **What remedy does the text suggest for one of the hazards in particular? Make notes in the fourth column of the chart above.**

6 **What do you think is the most important piece of advice the *Health* section gives to someone who reads it before they go to New Zealand?**

E X tra practice

What do you think a guidebook would say about the health hazards in your country? Look at a guidebook – preferably in English – and check your ideas.

B Top Tips: Healthy Travel Advice

1 While you are waiting at the medical centre one day, you pick up a leaflet *Top Tips: Healthy Travel Advice*. You skim the leaflet and notice the section headings opposite. Answer the questions.

   a Which of these topics were mentioned in the *Health* section of the guidebook (on page 15)?

   ----

   b Which sections of this leaflet do you think will be most useful to someone who is going to New Zealand?

   ----

2 Before you read the leaflet, think about what you already know about DVT.

3 Read the section of the leaflet about DVT. Check your answer to Exercise 2.

4 Skim the section again. Is it about precautions or is it about remedies?

1 Food and Water
2 Sun Protection
3 Accidents and Crime
4 Prevention of Insect Bites
5 Animal Bites
6 Deep Vein Thrombosis (DVT)

Deep Vein Thrombosis (DVT)

DVT is a serious condition where blood clots develop in the deep veins of the legs. There is some evidence that long-haul flights, especially when passengers have little or no exercise, may increase the risk of developing DVT.

There are ways you can reduce the possible risk of DVT on long-haul flights:

● Be comfortable in your seat

● Bend and straighten your legs, feet and toes while seated every half-hour or so during the flight

● Pressing the balls of your feet down hard against the floor or foot-rest will also help increase the blood flow in your legs and reduce clotting

● Take occasional short walks, when inflight advice suggests this is safe

● Take advantage of refuelling stopovers where it may be possible to get off the plane and walk about

● Drink plenty of water

● Be sensible about alcohol, which in excess leads to dehydration and immobility

● Avoid taking sleeping pills, which also cause immobility

Did you know ...?

DVT is an initialism – an abbreviation consisting of the first letter of each word, and in which each letter is pronounced. Another medical initialism is *NHS* – which is short for 'National Health Service'. Other short forms are acronyms – abbreviations consisting of the first letter of each word, and which can be pronounced as a word. The most commonly used medical acronym is *AIDS* – which is short for 'Acquired Immune Deficiency Syndrome'.

E ✗ tra practice

Go to the NHS website www.nhsdirect.nhs.uk if you want to find out more about DVT.

5 Follow the instructions from the inflight magazine below and do the exercises. Are any of them similar to those in the leaflet?

YOUR INFLIGHT EXERCISES

A few simple exercises can help reduce tiredness, stiffness and the likeliness of sluggish circulation, all of which can result from sitting in one place for a long time. The possibility of circulatory problems, particularly traveller's thrombosis, can be reduced by limiting the length of time you sit still. We advise you to carry out these exercises every couple of hours and take a brief walk around the cabin whenever you can.

1 **ANKLE CIRCLES**

Sit tall in your seat. Place the pillow under your right thigh, just above the knee. Keep your weight even. Now circle your right foot around, keeping the whole leg as still as possible. Make 10 circles in each direction with each foot.

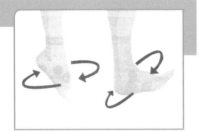

2 **CALF EXERCISE**

Still sitting tall, take your foot back underneath the seat a little, keeping your foot in line with the knee. Keeping your foot flat, push the toes and balls of your foot onto the floor, hold for a count of five, then release. Now push your heel into the floor for a count of five, release. Repeat these two actions with the knee at a right angle and with the leg stretched out a little. You should feel the work deep in your calf.

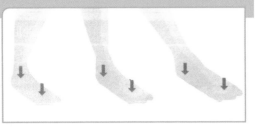

3 **STANDING**

Stand tall, feet parallel and hip-width apart. Come up onto your toes. Think tall as you lower your heels back down. Bend your knees so that they are directly over the centre of each foot. Your heels should stay down, and your feet should not roll in or out. Try not to stick your bottom out, or tuck it under. Slowly straighten your legs to return to the start position. Repeat 10 times.

Class bonus

Work in pairs. Think of some instructions for another exercise – for the neck or shoulders, or for a good sitting position, for example. Read out your instructions to the rest of the class. Carry out other students' instructions.

Can-do checklist

Tick what you can do.

	Can do	Need more practice
I can skim a text from a guidebook in order to get a general impression.	✓	
I can appreciate health risks and the precautions which I need to take.		✓
I can follow instructions and carry out exercises.		✓

Unit3
Our flight's delayed

Get ready to read

- Look at the title of this unit. Why might a flight be delayed? Tick ✓ the boxes.
  a There's a strike by airline staff. ☐
  b The plane has engine trouble. ☐
  c The incoming plane hasn't arrived. ☐
  d Security staff need to remove someone's luggage from the hold. ☐
  e There are bad weather conditions. ☐

- Have any of the things above ever happened to you?

- What is the difference between *cancel*, *curtail* and *postpone* a holiday? Read what three people say and complete the sentences with these words.
  a My mother went into hospital while I was in Dubai, so I had to come home early. I had to .... my holiday.
  b I broke my leg two weeks before we were due to go on a skiing holiday, so we didn't go. We had to .... our holiday.
  c I wanted to go skiing in December, but there wasn't enough snow. I'm now going in February. I had to .... my holiday.

- Have you ever had to cancel, postpone or curtail a holiday? Why?

go to Useful language p. 83

A We're staying at Heathrow

1 **Pierre and his wife Sophie are going on holiday. Look at Pierre's e-ticket. Circle the answers to these questions.**

a	Where are they going?	London	Cape Town
b	Which date are they travelling?	11th June	27th August
c	What time is their flight?	19.20	21.25
d	Which airline are they flying with?	BA	LHR

BRITISH AIRWAYS ➤   DUPLICATE   0001 OF 0001

E-TICKET RECEIPT / ITINERARY   DATE: 11JUN20_

NAME: DESCHAMPS/PIERRE MR (ADT)

FROM	TO	FLIGHT	CL	DATE	TIME	ST
BAG						
LONDON LHR	CAPE TOWN INTER	BA 0059	V	27 AUG	1920	OK

Learning tip

Texts may often contain words that you have not met before. (This can also happen in your own language.) Try not to use your dictionary every time you come across a new word. The word might not be important in terms of extracting the message from the text – so you can ignore it. Alternatively, you may be able to work out its meaning from related words or from the context – the words around it. Try to get into the habit of only using the dictionary as a last resort – or to check that you guessed the meaning correctly.

2 **Unfortunately for Pierre and Sophie, their plane did not reach its destination. They were given the letter on the opposite page when they got off the plane. Scan the letter and underline the information in the text that answers these questions. Do not use a dictionary to look up any unknown words.**

a Who is the letter to and from?
b Why didn't the plane reach its destination?
c Where was the plane when the letter was handed out?

Did you know ...?

The 24-hour clock is usually used in timetables. In the 24-hour clock, 2.15 pm (quarter past two in the afternoon) is written 14:15 and is pronounced 'fourteen fifteen'. 6 pm is written 18:00 and is pronounced 'eighteen hundred hours'. Some countries use the 24-hour clock in all situations.

BA0059 to Cape Town

BRITISH AIRWAYS

27TH AUGUST

Dear Customer

1 I am sorry for the disruption to your journey today. When flying over Morocco, your aircraft diverted to Barcelona with a medical emergency. Consequently the cabin crew are legally out of flying hours to continue on to Cape Town. The service has therefore returned to Heathrow to allow for a change of crew.

2 Your new departure time will be 18:00 on 28th August, arriving in Cape Town at 06:40 on 29th August.

3 We have arranged accommodation for you at the Renaissance Hotel. Breakfast, lunch and a three-minute telephone call will also be provided for you.

4 We suggest that you take your hold luggage with you when you go to the hotel. For your transport to the hotel, you will need to make your way to bus stop 15. This is located outside the main Terminal building.

5 Transport back to Heathrow Terminal 4 has been arranged for 14:15hrs. Please ensure you and your personal items are ready in the hotel lobby.

6 Check-in will be available on Zone A from 15:00hrs. Passengers travelling in First or Club World may check-in at Zone D or the First check-in zone immediately adjacent.

7 I don't underestimate the inconvenience and frustration you have been caused. I can assure you we are doing our best to make your wait as comfortable and brief as possible. Thank you very much for your understanding.

Yours faithfully
Reg Harper
Customer Service Duty Manager

PO Box 10 Heathrow Airport
Hounslow Middlesex TW6 2JA Tel 0181 562
Telex 8813983 BAWYSC G Cables Britishair

3 If you are 'out of work', you do not have a job. If a machine is 'out of order', it does not work. What do you think 'out of flying hours' (paragraph 1) means?

4 Read the rest of the letter and <u>underline</u> the information in the text that answers these questions. Again, do not use a dictionary to look up any unknown words.

a What arrangements have been made for the passengers to reach their destination?
b Where will they stay in the meantime?
c What should they do before they go there?
d How will they get to and from this place?

5 Passengers will get two meals at the hotel. Answer these questions.

a What else has the airline paid for?
----
b Why do you think they have arranged this facility?
----

6 Here are six words (in *italics*) from the letter that you may not know. Find the words in the letter and try to work out their meanings. Look at the questions next to each word below to help you.

a *disruption* (paragraph 1) – Look at the the letters *dis* at the beginning of the word. Do they have a positive or negative meaning? Did the flight continue to its destination as expected?
b *service* (paragraph 1) – Which words earlier in the letter could be described as the *service*?
c *lobby* (paragraph 5) – Look at the phrase *in the lobby*. This suggests part of the hotel. Where do people meet if they are going to leave a hotel?
d *inconvenience* (paragraph 7) – Do you think the prefix *in* is positive or negative?
e *frustration* (paragraph 7) – How else would you feel if your flight was delayed 22 hours?
f *brief* (paragraph 7) – Do you think this means *long* – or the opposite of *long*?

7 Which of the words in Exercise 6 did you need to know in order to extract the message from the letter?

Class bonus

Flight 0059 was delayed 22 hours in total. What effect would this have on both the passengers and the airline? Discuss the question in pairs. Then compare your ideas with the class. How many things can you think of?

B Are we covered?

1 **Some friends are talking about their holiday preparations. Read what the people said. Which of the things (a–c) are they checking? Tick ✓ the correct box.**

> I've got cover for winter sports.

> If I lose my passport, I can make a claim.

> According to the policy, I'm covered for delays and curtailment.

a their accommodation ☐
b their tickets ☐
c their insurance ☐

2 **Pierre and Sophie's flight is leaving 22 hours later than its scheduled departure time. They want to find out if they can make a claim on their insurance for this. Which section of their insurance policy should they look at? Circle the part of the policy below.**

Section of cover	Up to Limit of (£) per Insured Person	Excess*	Section
Cancellation of trip	£5,000	£50 (£15 for loss of deposit)	Section 1
Curtailment of trip	£5,000	£50	Section 2
Missed departure	£750	Nil	Section 3
Travel delay and Abandonment	£100	£50 (Abandonment only)	Section 4
Personal accident	Death £15,000 Loss of Limb(s) and sight £25,000	Nil	Section 5
Medical emergency expenses	£5,000,000	£50	Section 6

*Excess: certain sections of cover are subject to an excess applying to each claim. An excess means that you are responsible for the first sum per person per incident when you claim.

3 **Read the *You are covered* section of the policy on the opposite page. Answer the questions.**

a How much might they be able to claim?

----

b Is the cause of their delay mentioned as one of the causes that is covered?

----

4 **Read the *You are not covered* section of the policy on the opposite page. Answer the questions.**

a What would Pierre and Sophie need to have if they decided to make a claim?

----

b Have they already got this?

----

c Do you think Pierre and Sophie will make a claim?

Focus on ...
ways of travelling

1 Match the words in the box with their definitions.

| crossing | flight | journey | trip |

a the act of travelling somewhere and coming back
b travelling across water
c travelling by plane
d the act of travelling from one place to another

2 Complete these sentences with the four words above.
a My .... to work takes half an hour.
b My .... was cancelled because of the air traffic controllers' strike.
c Paul's just come back from a business .... to Saudi Arabia.
d The .... only takes ten minutes – we'll be on the island very soon.

3 Circle the correct word in these sentences.
a My parents went on a three-week *tour / trek* of Peru.
b Our class went on an *excursion / expedition* to London last week.
c My brother sometimes gives me a *drive / ride* to work.
d My grandparents visited many places on their Caribbean *cruise / voyage*.

Travel Delay and Abandonment

This section does not apply to trips within your Home Country.

YOU ARE COVERED

1 For a benefit of £20 for the first full 12 hours you are delayed and £10 for each full 12 hours you are delayed after that, up to a maximum of £100 (regardless of the number of incidents of delay) or
2 up to the amount under the cancellation section of this policy (less £50 excess) if you abandon the trip (on the outward journey only) after the first full 12 hours:
If your outward or return flights, sea crossing, coach or train departure to or from your Home Country, are delayed for more than 10 hours beyond the intended departure time (as specified on your travel ticket) as a result of:
  a) strike or industrial action (providing that when this policy was taken out, there was no reasonable expectation that the trip would be affected by such cause)
  b) adverse weather conditions
  c) mechanical breakdown or technical fault of the aircraft, coach, train or sea vessel

YOU ARE NOT COVERED

1 for the first £50 of each and every incident per each insured person involved in the incident (this is only applicable if you abandon the trip);
2 if you do not check-in for the flights, sea crossing, coach or train departure before the intended departure time;
3 if you do not obtain written confirmation from the airline, shipping, coach or train company stating the period and the reason for the delay.
4 for any claims arising from withdrawal from service temporarily or otherwise of the aircraft, coach, train or sea vessel on the orders or recommendation of the Civil Aviation Authority or a Port Authority or similar body in any Country.

5 Some passengers on the plane were going to a wedding in Cape Town on the 28th and another to a business meeting. They decided not to travel to South Africa because they would miss these events. Look at the table in Exercise 2. What should they be able to claim from this insurance policy?

----

6 Pierre and Sophie want to find out about making a claim. Read the *Claims procedures* part of the policy. Why did they abandon their plan to make a claim?

CLAIMS PROCEDURES

First, check this wording to make sure your claim is valid:
Travel Delay
Written confirmation must be obtained from the airline, shipping, coach or train company stating the period of the delay and the reason for the delay.
Please remember that cover for travel delay is provided for these specific reasons only:
· strike or industrial action (provided that when this policy was taken out and/or when the trip was booked, there was no reasonable expectation that the trip would be affected by such cause)
· adverse weather conditions
· the mechanical breakdown or technical fault of the aircraft, coach or sea vessel
Contact the Claims Service for a claim form on 0870 720 0807 when you return home.

E X tra practice

Look at the British Airways website www.ba.com and find out who exactly can buy British Airways travel insurance.

Can-do checklist

Tick what you can do.

	Can do	Need more practice
I can work out the meaning of words from their context – and from other similar words I know.		
I can find out flight details from a ticket and rearranged details from a letter.		
I can understand an insurance policy and consider whether to make a claim.		

Unit 4
I've been burgled

Get ready to read

- How much do you know about crime? Match the crimes in the box with the definitions in the chart below and write them in the first column.

  burglary   mugging   robbery   pickpocketing   shoplifting   smuggling

- Add one more crime and its definition to the chart.

- Complete the chart with the related words for the criminal and the verbs.

definition	crime	criminal	verb
a stealing something from a shop	shoplifting	shoplifter	
b stealing from a person or a place			
c stealing from someone's pocket			
d taking something illegally into another country			
e stealing from someone's home			
f attacking someone and stealing from them in a public place			
g			

go to Useful language p. 83

A Victims of crime

1 **Justyna Adamczak was burgled on 9th June. Three days later she received the letter on the opposite page. Who is it from?**

2 **Match each paragraph with its purpose (a–d). Write the paragraph numbers in the boxes.**

   a   explains what the police will do about the crime ☐
   b   encourages the assistance of the victim of the crime ☐
   c   offers support and sources of crime-related information ☐
   d   gives information related to the specific crime ☐

Learning tip

Punctuation is used in writing to divide up groups of words and make them easier to read. When speaking, you vary the speed and loudness of the words and add pauses. In writing, punctuation marks show these variations. Each punctuation mark is used for its own particular purpose; they can help you to predict what is coming next in a text. Paying attention to punctuation can help you to read more efficiently.

Did you know …?

The object of the verb *steal* is the thing which is taken away, e.g. *Two cars were stolen from outside the house. They stole my computer.* The object of the verb *rob* is the person or place from which things are stolen, e.g. *My neighbour was robbed last week. A gang of men robbed the bank.*

3 **The punctuation marks below are all in the letter. Match the punctuation marks with their uses in the letter. (One punctuation mark has more than one use.)**

   a . (full stop)   to add extra information
   b , (comma)   to end a sentence
   c : (colon)   to mark the beginning and
   d ; (semi-colon)   end of the title
   e ( ) (brackets)   to introduce a name/number
   f ' ' (quotation marks)   to separate items in a list
                                 to separate two parts of a
                                    sentence

4 **Imagine you are talking to a friend over the phone. Read the letter aloud, paying attention to its punctuation.**

Focus on ...
the passive

1 Complete these sentences from the text with passive verbs.
   a The crime _____is being_____ investigated (paragraph 1)
   b you _____ contacted (paragraph 3)
   c If no one _____ identified (paragraph 3)
   d your report _____ held (paragraph 3)
   e such crimes _____ (constantly) analysed (paragraph 3)
   f your case _____ reopened (paragraph 3)

2 Rephrase the sentences with verbs in the active form.
   a _C4794 Howson is investigating the crime_
   b _____
   c _____
   d _____
   e _____
   f _____

THAMES VALLEY POLICE

Crime Incident Management Unit
Thames Valley Police
Cowley Police Station
Oxford Road
Cowley
Oxford OX4 2LE

Tel: 08458 504405
12 June 20_
Ms Justyna Adamczak
61 Dove Close
Oxford
OX2 7GB

Dear Ms Adamczak

1 The crime that you recently reported (reference number: BL1194953/06) is being investigated by C14794 DAWSON. Please quote this reference number in any future calls or correspondence.

2 I have enclosed a copy of the 'Victims of Crime' leaflet, which you may find useful. If you have any further questions on crime prevention, victim support or the Criminal Justice System, or you would like to know more about Thames Valley Police, please use our contact number or visit the following websites:
www.thamesvalley.police.uk   www.crimereduction.gov.uk
www.cjsonline.gov.uk   0845 8 504 405

3 We will follow all reasonable lines of enquiry in an effort to identify the person(s) responsible for the crime you have suffered. In the event of any significant developments, such as an arrest, you will be contacted again and given an update. If, after an initial investigation, no one has been identified, your report will be held on file as an undetected crime and you will receive no further correspondence. However, such crimes are constantly analysed for links with new crimes and your case will be reopened should any new leads come to light.

4 Thank you for the time and trouble you have taken to contact us. All reported crime helps us to properly analyse criminal activity and target police resources more effectively. Please telephone us if you become aware of any further information that may assist us in our investigations; the police enquiry centres are open 24 hours a day.

Yours sincerely

Supervisor: Andrew Newton
Oxford Crime Incident Management Unit

---

5 **Justyna emails a friend and tells her what has happened since the burglary. Complete her email with the phrases a–f below. Write the numbers in the boxes.**

> New Message
> File Edit View Insert Format Tools Message Help
>
> The police sent me a letter. They gave me a reference number [1] They sent me a leaflet, which is for victims of crime, [2] They said that they would do what they could to catch the burglar [3] If they don't catch anyone, [4] They told me that they would reopen the case [5] They thanked me for reporting the burglary [6]

a and gave me some useful website addresses. ☐
b and would let me know of any developments. ☐
c if anything turned up. ☐
d they'll file the case as an undetected crime. ☐
e and told me to get in touch if I had any more information. ☐
f and the name of the officer who's looking after my case. ☐

6 **Have you ever been burgled, or do you know anyone who has? What was stolen?**

B Beat the burglar

1 Justyna phoned the police and asked for crime prevention advice. They sent her a brochure called *Beat the burglar.* The brochure has four parts: *Windows, Doors, Around the home* and *Don't forget.* Before you read the brochure, answer the questions.

a What do you think is the aim of the brochure?

----

b What kind of things do you think each part of the brochure will mention?

----

2 You are going to read the *Don't forget* part of the brochure. Skim the article, looking at the headings and the visuals only. Which two sections are most likely to be about the prevention of crime?

Did you know ...?

Dashes (–) can be used instead of commas, brackets or semi-colons; you won't usually find dashes in formal writing, however. They are often used to reflect the way we speak.

3 Scan the text and check your answer to Exercise 2. What are the other sections about?

4 Circle the word *property* (four times) in the section *Postcode your property.* The word *property* can refer to both a building or to things that belong to someone. Answer these questions.

a What does *property* refer to in the first section?

----

b Which other words in the brochure – either singular or plural – have a meaning which is similar to *property*?

DON'T FORGET

POSTCODE YOUR PROPERTY

In only 9% of cases where something has been stolen is property returned.

Marked property can deter burglars because it's harder for a thief to sell and can help the police to return it if found.

■ Mark items with an indelible identification – showing your postcode and the number of your house or flat or the first two letters of its name – using a permanent etching tool or an ultraviolet marker pen. Only use UV marking when other methods would reduce the value of the object – because the mark can fade.

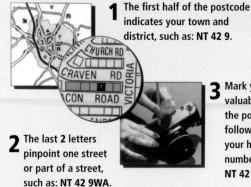

1 The first half of the postcode indicates your town and district, such as: **NT 42 9.**

2 The last 2 letters pinpoint one street or part of a street, such as: **NT 42 9WA.**

3 Mark your valuables using the postcode followed by your house number such as **NT 42 9WA 7.**

5 The brochure contains a mixture of information, facts and advice. Read the brochure carefully and <u>underline</u> everything it tells you to do. For example:

■ <u>Mark items with an indelible identification</u> – showing your postcode and the number of your house or flat or the first two letters of its name – using a permanent etching tool or an ultraviolet marker pen. Only use UV marking when other methods would reduce the value of the object – because the mark can fade.

6 One section of the brochure does not actually tell you what to do. Which section? Write your own advice for this section.

----

7 Which of the recommendations in the brochure would you take up?

Take pictures of all valuable items like jewellery and silverware and write down the serial numbers of your TV, video, hi-fi, home computer and camera equipment, to help the police identify them should they be recovered. If you have many valuable items, fit a safe.

Ask your local police station for 'postcoded property' stickers to display in the front and back windows of your house.

INSURANCE

Insurance will relieve you of the financial worry of replacing stolen goods and many insurance companies offer reduced premiums for people with good home security. The firm should tell you if it minds which systems you buy.

SMOKE DETECTORS

With all security, consideration must be given to the risk of fire and means of escape. Fit a smoke detector – a minimum of one per floor – installed to the manufacturer's instructions.

BE A GOOD NEIGHBOUR

If you see anyone acting suspiciously in your neighbourhood, call the police. There are now over 130,000 Neighbourhood Watch Schemes in this country – why not join one? Anyone can start up a Watch – call your police for details.

IF YOU ARE BURGLED

A secure home will reduce the chance of you getting burgled. But, if you get home and notice signs of a break-in:

- Don't go in or call out – the intruder could still be inside.
- Go to a neighbour's house to call the police.

CRIME PREVENTION ADVICE

All police forces have officers trained in crime prevention – contact your local station for advice. Some forces can arrange surveys of your home or business premises and recommend security improvements. This is a popular service – if there's a waiting list, you may be sent an information pack so that you can do your own survey.

Class bonus

Look at the advice you underlined in Exercise 5. Write a follow-up question for each piece of advice, e.g. *How should you mark items with an indelible identification?* Then work with a partner and ask each other your questions.

E X tra practice

You can find lots of information about how to prevent crime on the Internet, from staying safe on public transport to keeping your internet transactions private. Go to www.homeoffice.gov.uk for some ideas. You can also find out about Neighbourhood Watch on www.crimereduction.gov.uk.

Can-do checklist

Tick what you can do.

	Can do	Need more practice
I can understand a letter from the police.		
I can interpret punctuation and use it to read a text efficiently.	✓	✓
I can separate information and advice, and follow advice about protecting my home.		

Unit5
Picasso's birthplace

Get ready to read

○ Look at the photograph. This shows the artist Pablo Picasso. How much do you know about him? Complete the sentences with *France* or *Spain*.
  a He was born in _____ .
  b He grew up in _____ .
  c He spent all his adult life in _____ .
  d He died in _____ .

○ What else do you know about Picasso? Write two sentences.

  _____

  _____

go to Useful language p. 84

A Picasso museums

1 **A friend of yours has just been on a trip to Málaga. This is what she said about one of the museums there. Does she recommend a visit?**

a *It's open* all day – which is very convenient. I went about two o'clock.

b *I looked around for a while*, then I had something to eat, and then I went to some more galleries.

c *It didn't cost* much to get in – just a few euros.

d *You can see* lots of Picasso's works there – and not just paintings.

e *The building dates from* the sixteenth century.

f *The building itself is* worth a visit. It's beautiful – and enormous!

g *Picasso's family have given* some of his works to the museum.

h *I learned a lot about* Picasso at that museum. It was very interesting!

2 **Look at this description of a museum in Málaga. Is it the museum your friend was talking about in Exercise 1?**

Fundación Municipal Pablo Ruiz Picasso
Plaza de la Merced, 15
🕐(Mon–Sat 10 am–2 pm & 5–8 pm, Sun 10 am–2 pm; free)

Situated in the historic Plaza de la Merced, the house where Picasso was born has been converted into a study centre about the life and works of the painter and is visited by thousands of people every year. It provides interesting information about the childhood and the work of Picasso.

A replica of the Picasso family's living accommodation: The first floor of the house where Picasso was born contains a museum with works by the artist and his father, José Ruiz Blasco, and personal items belonging to the Ruiz Picasso family which have been donated by the painter's relatives. Among the articles of interest are Pablo Picasso's christening gown and pieces of furniture from the years 1880–1884, the period when the family lived in this house. The building was constructed in 1861 and was number 36.

3 **Why did this particular building become a museum? Underline the answer in the text.**

4 Look at this description of another museum. Is this the museum your friend was talking about in Exercise 1?

Picasso Museum Málaga

Palacio de Buenavista. San Agustin, 8
(Tues–Thurs 10 am–8 pm, Fri & Sat 10 am–9 pm,
Sun 10 am–8 pm; permanent collection €6, temporary
collection €4.50, combined ticket for both €8;
www.museopicassomalaga.org)

The Picasso Museum of Málaga is currently displaying more than three hundred works which range through the painter's artistic career, as well as different techniques and styles, which enable the visitor to gain a great insight into his work. The Picasso Museum is located in the Palacio de Buenavista, a building of great beauty featuring Andalucian Renaissance architecture, which came to fruition thanks to donations from Christine and Bernard Ruiz Picasso, the artist's daughter-in-law and grandson.

The permanent collection contains 204 works, including oils, etchings, drawings and ceramics, ranging from the 19th century up to 1972. The best-known are 'Retrato de Paulo con gorro blanco', dedicated to the artist's first child, whose birth inspired his neoclassic style after the Cubist period, and 'Olga Kokhlova con mantilla', which is a portrait of his first wife wearing a Spanish mantilla (shawl), and which is considered to be one of his best works.

'The Picassos of Antibes' (until 11th June) This exhibition, on display for the first time in Spain, includes 73 works from the Musée Picasso Antibes (Antibes, France) carried out by the artist after the Second World War.

The Buenavista Palace was declared a national monument in 1939 and is situated right in the historic centre of the city. Among the museum's facilities are a library, an auditorium, a document centre and a cafeteria. The magnificent Mudejar artistry of the Palace, its Renaissance and Baroque ceilings and its fantastic view are more excellent reasons to visit the museum, which covers an overall area of 8,300 square metres.

5 Read the sentences in Exercise 1 again. Underline the evidence in the text which supports the statements.

6 Imagine you have visited the *Fundación Municipal Pablo Ruiz Picasso*. Use the words in *italics* in the sentences in Exercise 1 to begin sentences about the *Fundación Municipal Pablo Ruiz Picasso*. The text in Exercise 2 may not give you all the information you need, so you will have to use your imagination.

a It's open from 10 am to 2 pm every day and then from 5 pm to 8 pm Monday to Saturday.

Learning tip

Writers do not always state facts directly, so readers have to infer them (work them out) for themselves using the clues available. Think about the words you are reading, and ask yourself 'So, what does this tell me?'.

7 Look at these statements about Pablo Picasso. What evidence is there in the texts to support the statements?

a Picasso was born in 1881. Picasso was born in the Fundación Municipal Pablo Ruiz Picasso. His family lived there from 1880–1884, so he was born sometime in this period.
b Picasso died in 1973. _____
c Picasso's father was a painter. _____
d Picasso's first wife wasn't Spanish. _____
e Picasso had more than one child. _____
f Picasso visited the south of France in 1946. _____

8 What else can you infer about Picasso and his life from the texts?

9 Would you be interested in visiting either of these museums?

Did you know ...?

The *Picasso Museum Málaga* and the *Fundación Municipal Pablo Ruiz Picasso* are not the only Picasso museums in Spain – there is another one in Barcelona. Picasso moved there with his family in 1895 and put on his first public exhibition two years later. Picasso's most famous painting *Guernica* is in the *Reina Sofia Gallery* in Madrid.

B Picasso's return

1 What do you know about Pablo Picasso's early life?

2 You are going to read a text from a tourist brochure about Málaga. The text is called *Picasso's return*. What do you think the text might be about?

3 Skim the text and check your answer to Exercise 2. What else does the text aim to do?

Picasso's return

José Antonio del Cañizo

If Picasso were to come back and visit the people of Málaga, all dressed up in his Breton fisherman's jersey, his shorts and espadrilles, he would fly over Málaga, shouting with surprise at all the changes which have taken place since he left here in January 1901, at the age of 19.

No doubt he would make an impeccable vertical landing straight down into the *Plaza de la Merced* (Square of Mercy) to have a look at the house where he was born, currently the seat of the *Fundación Municipal Pablo Ruiz Picasso* (1). Burning with impatience, he would run around among the cars, the girls, the voices and the orange trees until he reached the Picasso Museum (2). And he would surely run down to the beach, longing to see again that blinding sky and shimmering sea, whose dreamy surface inspired in him such disconcerting dreamy images when he was a boy.

But those eyes, eyes that have seen far beyond what others see, would open wider on discovering a magic tropical forest had been planted right beside the port, exactly where the land was beginning to gain ground over the sea when he said goodbye to Málaga. He would become submerged in this fascinating Park (3), amazed, thinking that if only he had seen it before he left, he would have included some of its blazing images in his paintings.

Now he would run round again, rubbing his hands, trying to make up for all the lost time. After passing in front of the *Diputación Provincial* (Provincial Council) (4), he would be so hungry for the sights of Málaga that he would run straight on to *Calle Larios* (5), a street he knew when it was still brand new and which he would now find completely redesigned and full of life; a newly created *Plaza de la Constitución* (Constitution Square) (6) full of people enjoying themselves and presided over by a beautiful Genoese fountain; and then on to the Cathedral and its Museum (7).

His attractive and very varied walk around Málaga would be further enriched by a visit to the *Alcazaba* (Castle) (8) and the *Palacio de La Aduana* (Customs House), now the *Subdelegación del Gobierno* (Government Office) (9), with a museum housing paintings by his father and by Muñoz Degrain, his maestro. And then on to the Noble Hospital (10), which he had seen as a boy and which now hosts the City Hall's Environment Office, which looks after Málaga Park and all the other Green Zones in Malaga.

He would surely feel especially excited when he came to the *Plaza de Toros* (Bullring) (11) with its Bullfighting Museum named after Antonio Ordóñez, where he would recall that his first oil painting was precisely of a scene during a bullfight, and that both he and Antonio had drawn – one in the air and the other on paper and canvas – the most agile and graceful lines of the art of bullfighting.

Finally, drunk after so much Málaga and drugged with nostalgia and the scent of jasmine, he would climb up to *Castillo de Gibralfaro* (Gibralfaro Castle) (12) and drink in the whole city from above, as he so often used to do as a young boy. And he would end his enchanting walk with a tasty local meal, by the end of which he would have decided that Málaga is definitely a place to come back to stay.

4 (Circle) the places mentioned in the text and draw the route on the map.

5 In the first paragraph, we are told that a lot of changes have taken place since Picasso left Málaga. Read the text carefully and find the following.

a two places which did not exist when Picasso left Málaga

----

b four places whose use has changed since Picasso left Málaga

----

----

c two places whose appearance has changed since Picasso left Málaga

----

----

6 What else do you learn about Picasso – both his art and his life – from this text?

E✗**tra practice**

Find out more about the life of Pablo Picasso by looking in the library or on the Internet.

Class bonus

Play a memory game. How many different ways can you end the sentence: *If Picasso were to return to Málaga, … ?*

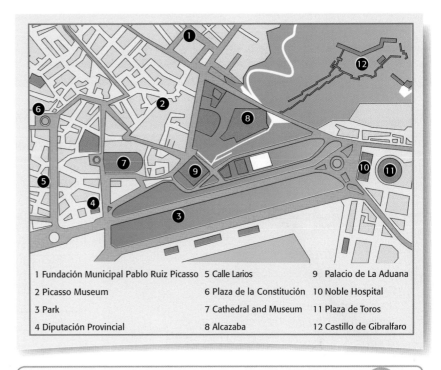

1 Fundación Municipal Pablo Ruiz Picasso 5 Calle Larios   9 Palacio de La Aduana

2 Picasso Museum   6 Plaza de la Constitución 10 Noble Hospital

3 Park   7 Cathedral and Museum 11 Plaza de Toros

4 Diputación Provincial   8 Alcazaba   12 Castillo de Gibralfaro

Focus on ...

the second conditional

ab**C**def

1 There are lots of second conditional verbs in this text, e.g. *If Picasso were to come back and visit … he would fly, he would make, he would run*. When do we use this verb form? Tick ✓ the correct answer.
   a to talk about a real possibility in the present ☐
   b to talk about an unlikely or impossible event in the present ☐
   c to talk about something that did not happen in the past ☐

2 Complete these sentences about Picasso with the second conditional form of a verb.
   a If he _____ in the Plaza de la Merced, he _____ voices.
   b If he _____ down to the beach, he _____ the sea.
   c If he _____ to Plaza de la Constitución, he _____ himself.
   d If he _____ up to Castillo de Gibralfaro, he _____ down on the city.

3 Write sentences about a place you once knew. Begin with *If I were to go back and visit … .*

Can-do checklist

Tick what you can do.

	Can do	Need more practice
I can infer meaning when it is not stated directly.	✓	✓
I can find out about a museum and decide whether or not to visit it.		✓
I can follow a route.		

Unit 6
Love it or loathe it!

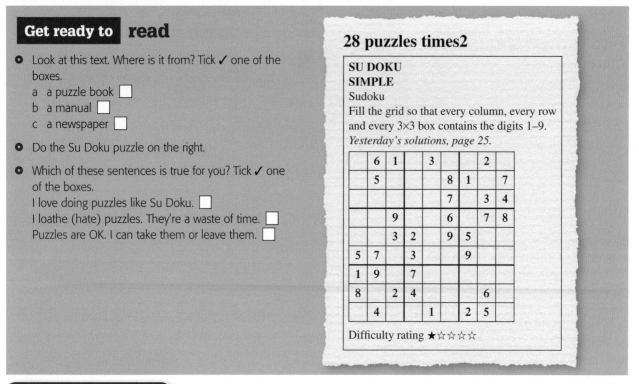

Get ready to read

- Look at this text. Where is it from? Tick ✓ one of the boxes.
  - a a puzzle book ☐
  - b a manual ☐
  - c a newspaper ☐

- Do the Su Doku puzzle on the right.

- Which of these sentences is true for you? Tick ✓ one of the boxes.
  - I love doing puzzles like Su Doku. ☐
  - I loathe (hate) puzzles. They're a waste of time. ☐
  - Puzzles are OK. I can take them or leave them. ☐

28 puzzles times2

SU DOKU
SIMPLE
Sudoku
Fill the grid so that every column, every row and every 3×3 box contains the digits 1–9.
Yesterday's solutions, page 25.

	6	1		3			2	
	5				8	1		7
					7		3	4
		9			6		7	8
		3	2		9	5		
5	7		3			9		
1	9		7					
8		2	4				6	
	4			1		2	5	

Difficulty rating ★☆☆☆☆

go to Useful language p. 84

A The world beater

1 You are going to read the first two sections of an online article from *times2*, a supplement of the British newspaper *The Times*. The article is about Su Doku and it has the title *The world beater*. Which of these topics do you think is the main topic of the article? Tick ✓ one of the boxes.
   - a the origins and history of Su Doku ☐
   - b the global popularity of Su Doku ☐
   - c the rules of Su Doku ☐
   - d the Su Doku world championships ☐

2 Skim the article on the opposite page and check your answer to Exercise 1.

3 Skim the article again. Match the paragraphs with the topics below. Write the paragraph numbers in the boxes.
   - a reasons for the popularity of Su Doku ☐
   - b the speed with which Su Doku has become popular ☐
   - c examples of the impact of Su Doku in various countries ☐
   - d the availability of Su Doku puzzles ☐

4 A rhetorical question is a question that is asked in order to make a statement and which does not expect an answer. Which paragraph contains rhetorical questions?

5 Read each paragraph again more carefully. <u>Underline</u> the information which is given about each of the topics in Exercise 3.

TIMES ONLINE

http://www.timesonline.co.uk

The Times June 30, 2006

The world beater

RICHARD MORRISON

In the 600 days since *The Times* first published Su Doku, it has conquered the world. Our correspondent and Times writers worldwide report on its impact.

1 *Su who?* Was it only 20 months ago that this innocent quip first echoed around these offices? Only 600 days since *The Times* launched an unknown number puzzle on an unsuspecting public? Only 600 days since Wayne Gould's addictive grids began to nibble at our spare time, self-esteem, sang-froid, even our sanity? It seems unbelievable. Chess took 600 years to spread across the medieval world. Other pastimes – Aussie-rules football, Eton fives, morris dancing – wouldn't catch on if you gave them 600 centuries.

2 Yet in 600 days Su Doku has bewitched, bothered and bewildered populations across the globe. Tap those two little words into Google and you get 90 million hits. Peruse any bookshop and you find dozens of Su Doku manuals, some written as earnestly as philosophical tracts.

3 And, as our correspondents report here, pick up any number of newspapers on five continents and you find half a billion puzzlers getting a daily dose of nine-by-nines. Su Doku is huge in America and India – where Compulsive Su Doku syndrome is a recognised psychiatric complaint and beauty queens vie to complete puzzles on live TV. It appears in 60 Chinese papers and is a national craze in Japan, where a million people consider themselves *otaku*, or obsessives.

4 The secret of its allure? Su Doku is a game with very simple aims and rules, but limitless scope for complex ramifications and subtle strategies. But perhaps its phenomenal success really only proves that, whether in Bangkok or Baldock, people love to escape from the real world, with all its unresolvable dilemmas and random irritants, into a realm where reason rules supreme, and where every problem has a perfect solution – even if the process of finding it leaves us frothing with frustration.

6 **Find the following words and phrases in the text. Circle the correct answer for each question. Remember to read what comes before and after these words to help you answer the question.**

1 *Aussie-rules football, Eton fives, morris dancing*
What point is the author making about Su Doku when he mentions these three pastimes?
a They caught on as quickly as Su Doku.
b They took 60,000 years to catch on.
c They are little-known pastimes and will never catch on.

2 *some written as earnestly as philosophical tracts*
What point is the author making about Su Doku when he mentions manuals written in this way?
a philosophers are writing books about Su Doku
b Su Doku is being taken very seriously indeed
c you can find information about Su Doku in philosophy books

3 *whether in Bangkok or Baldock*
What point is the author making about Su Doku and its appeal when he mentions these two places?
a Su Doku is popular around the world
b Su Doku is very popular in two places with similar names
c these are the places where Su Doku is most popular

7 **How do you think Richard Morrison feels about Su Doku? Find two or three clues in the text.**

Did you know ...?

Although the name Su Doku is Japanese – roughly translating as 'Number Place' – the puzzle may have evolved from a simpler version which was created by Euler, the 18th-century Swiss mathematician. All the puzzles in *The Times* are created by Wayne Gould, a puzzle enthusiast and former Hong Kong judge. He came across Su Doku in a Tokyo bookshop, began making puzzles himself, and brought them to *The Times* – and to the rest of the world! Note that the American spelling is Sudoku (one word).

E X tra practice

Imagine you have to write a couple of paragraphs for this article about the impact of Su Doku in your country. Do some research on the Internet.

B Su Doku mind games

1 **You are going to read another article about Su Doku, this time from the American newspaper *USA Today*. This article is called *Sudoku mind games*. What do you think the article might be about?**

2 **Read the introduction to the article. What happened when Robert Lipsyte tried Su Doku?**

----

3 **Skim the article. Which paragraph describes what happened when Robert Lipsyte tried Su Doku for the first time?**

Focus on ... abcdef
the suffixes *-ful* and *-less*

1 You can add the suffix *-ful* (meaning 'with') to *forget* to make the word *forgetful* and the suffix *-less* (meaning 'without') to *mind* to make the word *mindless*. Can you add *-less* to *forget* and *-ful* to *mind*? Read the text and find out which one is possible.

2 Look at these words. Can you add *-ful* or *-less*? Or can you add both? Tick ✓ the boxes.

		-ful	-less
a	limit		
b	care		
c	wonder		
d	home		
e	colour		
f	stress		

Sudoku mind games

I tried the new puzzle craze. I was told that it would be stimulating and relaxing. What I didn't expect is that it would be life-changing (and not in a good way).

By Robert Lipsyte

Sudoku changed my life

1 They said my brain needed a game, something mindless and absorbing that would relax and stimulate. The mind is a muscle, they said; if you don't use it, you'll lose it. They said they knew everything.

2 A few years ago, I would have ignored them. But my mind has been tired and forgetful. I was wasting energy chewing over problems I couldn't solve, getting angry, jealous, wanting more. They had suggestions for me, as they always do, those psychologists, life coaches, social commentators with their 5/7/11 tips/ideas/lessons for a happier/hipper/healthier me.

3 Maybe they just didn't want me to think about the war, the polar icecaps, airport insecurity. Or maybe they really did know everything. So I listened when they said, "Try word puzzles." But I hated word puzzles because they are like tests, and most of them are too cutesy.

A bunch of numbers

4 I needed something truly mindless. Then they suggested Sudoku, a Japanese puzzle in which you arrange the numbers 1 through 9 in 81 squares so that no numbers repeat in any horizontal or vertical row. You don't even need to know words or arithmetic. Can you get more mindless than that?

5 I ran out and bought one of the books, *Sudoku for Dummies*, which had 240 puzzles graded from easy to tricky to tough and diabolical, based on the numbers already supplied.

6 I started with easy. That's when Sudoku began to change my life.

7 I was barely half-way through my first puzzle when it hit me – I hate this, too. It was not only mindless, it also was not absorbing, not relaxing or stimulating. It was a boring waste of time. If my mind is a muscle, I thought, I will lose it playing Sudoku. The first Sudoku was my last because I realized I didn't want something mindless. I wanted … mindful.

Better alternative

8 I ditched *Sudoku for Dummies* and found *Mindfulness in Plain English* by Henepola Gunaratan, a Buddhist abbot. I usually hate self-help books as passionately as I hate puzzles, but this one seemed jargon-free, and it promised that if I got serious about sitting quietly and setting my mind free for a few minutes a day, I might start seeing and then dispelling some of the greed, anger and jealousy in my life, and develop more compassion for myself and others. The abbot had my shortcomings nailed.

9 Meditation was much harder than I had anticipated. My mind wandered and got stuck on trying to thrash out personal problems. Counting breaths to bring it back took energy. I thought about the war, the polar icecaps and airport insecurity and had trouble shaking loose. I tried to let thoughts flow, to look at them without reacting, then send them on their way. It was days before I began to do so, weeks before I felt relaxed and stimulated after 20 minutes or so of meditating.

10 I'm not feeling smug about this because I am neither regular nor adequate at meditating. I think it will take a long time before I am able to transfer that mindfulness from a few minutes in the morning to an all-day way of life, maybe years before I start thinking more clearly.

11 But I do think I've come through the valley of mindlessness, where they wanted to send me. Was it because they had books/CDs/DVDs of tips/ideas/lessons to sell, or was it part of a larger plot to keep me from thinking about eliminating war and poverty, and cleaning up the environment and myself? Is Sudoku one of those weapons of mass distraction?

12 If that thought comes up in meditation some morning, I will let it slide through without wasting energy hating it as much as I used to hate puzzles.

Learning tip

Our purpose in reading a text is to understand the writer's message. This means understanding the words the writer uses and also understanding what the writer wants to do with these words. This could be presenting facts, describing a series of events, giving an opinion. Understanding a text requires us to work out the function of each sentence.

4 Skim the article again. Complete the sentences.

a Paragraphs _____ are about how Robert Lipsyte came to try Su Doku.

b Paragraphs _____ are about what happened after he tried it for the first time.

5 Answer the questions about how Robert Lipsyte came to try Su Doku.

a What has happened to him recently? _____

_____

b How does he describe himself and his mind? _____

_____

c What has he been worrying about? _____

_____

d Which game did he try first of all? _____

e How did he get on with this game? _____

f What was – in theory – the advantage of Su Doku over this game?

_____

6 What was Robert Lipsyte's reaction to Su Doku? Did he love it, like it or loathe it?

7 Look at the paragraphs which are about what happened after Robert Lipsyte tried Su Doku for the first time. Complete the sentences.

a Paragraph(s) _____ describe(s) events or facts.

b Paragraph(s) _____ give(s) his opinions.

c Paragraph(s) _____ include(s) both.

d Paragraph(s) _____ include(s) rhetorical questions.

8 Answer the questions about the rhetorical questions in the article.

a Who is 'they' in paragraph 11? Is this the same 'they' as in paragraphs 1–4 ?

b Why does Robert Lipsyte mention 'weapons of mass distraction'? What word usually finishes the expression 'weapons of mass'?

c Are there any other rhetorical questions in the article?

9 Robert Lipsyte mentions 'wasting energy' in the last paragraph. Answer the questions.

a In which context has he mentioned 'wasting energy' earlier?

b Why does he mention 'wasting energy' in the last paragraph?

10 How would you summarize the author's experiences and views? Why do you think he chose *Sudoku mind games* as the title for the article?

Class bonus

How typical do you think Robert Lipsyte's views are? How many people in your class share them?

Can-do checklist

Tick what you can do.

	Can do	Need more practice
I can relate the contents of an article to its title.	✓	✓
I can recognize rhetorical questions.		
I can read authentic newspaper articles and extract the main points.		
I can distinguish between opinions and facts.		

Review 1
Units 1–6

A Are these statements true (T) or false (F)?

1 After you have scanned a text to find a particular word, you might then read the text around the word. ...... (Unit 1)

2 If you skim a text, you will not know which parts of the text are worth reading again. ...... (Unit 2)

3 You do not always need to know the meaning of unknown words you come across when reading a text. ...... (Unit 3)

4 There is no need to pay attention to punctuation when you are reading; it does not serve much purpose. ...... (Unit 4)

5 Readers sometimes have to work out facts for themselves because writers do not always state everything directly. ...... (Unit 5)

6 If you want to understand a writer's message, then understanding the meaning of each individual word is all that is needed. ...... (Unit 6)

B Now read the *Learning tips* for Units 1–6 on pages 87–88. Do you want to change any of your answers in Exercise A?

1 Biting and stinging insects are, at best, a nuisance and at worst can cause serious problems. Malaria can be a problem in some countries, but now mosquitoes in the USA and Canada are passing on a different disease, West Nile virus, that can be equally unpleasant. So wherever you are going, pack a good insect repellent in your bag.

2 Repellents containing the chemical DEET are the most effective at keeping the mosquitoes away. Other ways to avoid mosquito bites include covering up with long sleeves, long trousers and socks when outdoors. Mosquitoes may bite through thin clothing, so spraying clothes with DEET will give extra protection.

3 The hours from dusk to dawn are peak mosquito biting times for many species of mosquitoes. Take extra care to use repellent and wear protective clothing during evening and early morning – or consider indoor activities during these times.

4 In your room at night, electrical plug-in repellents will slowly release insecticide to prevent bites while you are sleeping. A mosquito net will also offer protection if you are travelling somewhere where they can be suspended. Invest in a good quality mosquito net.

5 Ask your pharmacist for advice about suitable insect repellents and soothing creams to treat any bites or stings.

C Jorge is at the doctor's surgery and is reading a leaflet. Skim the text, which is from the leaflet. Answer these questions.

7 What is the title of the leaflet? Tick ✓ one of the boxes.
  a How to give up smoking ☐
  b Holiday health ☐
  c Hospital treatment for overseas visitors ☐

8 What is the best title for this text? Tick ✓ one of the boxes.
  a Malaria and other diseases ☐
  b Insect bites and stings ☐
  c Insect repellents ☐

D Match a heading with each of the five paragraphs. Write the letters in the boxes. (There are two extra headings.)

9 paragraph 1 ☐
10 paragraph 2 ☐
11 paragraph 3 ☐
12 paragraph 4 ☐
13 paragraph 5 ☐

a mosquito related illnesses
b the riskiest destinations
c the riskiest times
d getting advice
e natural remedies
f precautions to take
g what to do overnight

E Find words in the text which mean the following. There is one word in each paragraph.

14 something that annoys you or causes trouble ....

15 successful or achieving the results that you want ....

16 the time before night when it is not yet dark ....

17 hung up ....

18 make an injury less painful ....

F **Jorge is travelling to Canada to visit relatives there. Read the letter and answer the following questions.**

19 Who is the letter to?

----

20 Who is it from?

----

21 Where was Jorge when he received this letter?

----

22 When did he get the letter?

----

23 Why was his flight late?

G **CanAir Atlantic wants to repay passengers for the disruption of their flight. Jorge decides that he might take advantage of their offer. Are these sentences true (T) or false (F)?**

24 The cost of his next CanAir Atlantic flight will be $200 CAD. ☐

25 He can make his journey whenever he wants to. ☐

26 Taxes and surcharges will also be paid by CanAir Atlantic. ☐

27 If Jorge books online, he must make the trip before claiming a refund. ☐

28 The Refund Services need to see a copy of this letter in order to give a refund. ☐

29 If Jorge wanted to make a phone booking from London, he should use the phone number given in the letter. ☐

30 Jorge's brother could use the offer instead of Jorge himself. ☐

CanAir Atlantic

Gordon Macdonald
Manager, Customer Relations
Chef de service – Relations clientèle

21/07/20__

Dear Valued Customer

Reference: COEM10720
Please accept our sincere apology for the inconvenience you experienced during the disruption of your flight from Roissy to Toronto today (21/07/20__). If you have an onward connection from Toronto, our airport team here will do all possible to assist you to your final destination.

CanAir Atlantic takes pride in maintaining the safety and comfort of our passengers and crew. However, we do acknowledge that the technical delay you experienced at Roissy has upset your travel plans.

As a gesture of goodwill, we are pleased to provide you with a credit for future travel on CanAir Atlantic to the amount of $200.00 CAD. This credit is valid for one year from today and is transferable to another person of your choice (applicable charges and surcharges apply).

If booking on our website, we would be pleased to apply this credit upon completion of your next trip. Simply fax this letter and the itinerary/receipt from your trip to Refund Services Department at (204) 800-8927. If you choose to offer your credit to another customer, a signed letter giving your authorization must accompany the itinerary/receipt of the customer you are giving the credit to as well as this letter. CanAir Atlantic will then verify the name on the original credit. Alternatively, to apply the credit to a telephone booking in North America, please call 1-888-722-6668. If you are calling from elsewhere, consult www.canair.com/customerservices for our phone number and refer to the Reference number above.

Thank you for your patience and understanding. We hope your future travel with us will be more enjoyable.

Sincerely,

G Macdonald

Unit 7
Import, export!

go to Useful language p. 84

Get ready to read

- Write the names of the products in the photographs in the first column of the chart.

	product	import	export
a			
b			
c			
d			
e			

- Does your country import or export these goods? Or does it do both? Complete the chart.

A Please confirm

1 Ivo is a product manager for Globale Fleischimport AG, a meat importer in Basel, Switzerland. He is looking at some correspondence with a supplier in Goiania, Brazil. Read the emails on the opposite page and number them in the order in which they were received.

2 Find the two emails ending *Please consider* and *Please confirm* and underline the correct word in these sentences.

   a The *price / quantity* should be considered.
   b The *price / quantity* should be confirmed.

3 Imagine you are Ivo's assistant, and you need to check on the quantities and prices. Read the correspondence and answer these questions.

   a How much meat did Globale Fleischimport AG want to buy in total?

   b How much meat are they going to get in total?

   c How much did Globale Fleischimport AG want to pay for the meat?

   d How much are they going to have to pay?

   e Why is there a difference in the quantities and prices?

Learning tip

Understanding a text is a two-way process between writer and reader. It works best when the message is written clearly. Sometimes the reader lacks background knowledge of the subject, so the writer's message is not entirely clear. The reader may need to do some further reading or ask someone for clarification.

4 Read the correspondence again. Is there anything that is unclear? Make a list of questions you would like to ask Ivo or things you would like to check. Here are two examples.

   What are striploins?
   USD stands for US dollars, doesn't it?
   ....
   ....
   ....

Did you know ...?

It is said that more than 70% of the world's correspondence is written in English. Furthermore, nearly half of all business deals in Europe are conducted in English.

A ☐

Dear Carlos

Thanks for prompt reply. However, we cannot accept USD 5,000. Market is coming down slightly. We are prepared to book 500 kg weekly at USD 4,700. This is the level your competitors are quoting.

Please consider and reply.
Ivo

B ☐

Hi Ivo

We can offer striploins for shipment in weeks 34–37 at USD 5,000 per ton fob São Paulo Guarulhos. However, we can produce 500 kg per week maximum.

Best regards
Carlos

C ☐

Dear Carlos

We appreciate the good quality of Meat Corporation and accept quote. We herewith confirm 500 kg of striploins for shipment in weeks 34, 35, 36 and 37 at USD 4,900.

Best regards
Ivo

D ☐1

Dear Carlos

One of our customers is planning a promotion for striploins during the next month. Please quote following quantities:

500 kg for shipment in week 34
1,000 kg for shipment in week 35
500 kg for shipment in week 36
500 kg for shipment in week 37

Please note that production date must not be older than 6 days before shipment.

Looking forward to hearing from you.
Ivo

E ☐

Ivo,

4,700 is definitely too low. In order to keep business going we could accept USD 4,900. But this is really best we can do. Please confirm.

Carlos

5 Ivo's new assistant, Margrit, has some questions about the correspondence. Which of your questions in Exercise 4 has she asked below?

a Who is the customer that you mention?
b Striploins are from cows, are they?
c Presumably week 1 is the first week in January, is it?
d Does *shipment* mean that the meat will travel by ship?
e What does *fob* stand for?
f Why is the price quoted in tons, but the order quoted in kilograms?

6 Match Margrit's questions in Exercise 5 with Ivo's answers. Write the letters in the boxes.

☐e 1 It actually means 'free on board'. This is a commercial term which means that the goods are loaded on a vessel, in this case a plane in São Paulo.
☐ 2 It's traditional, I suppose. Normally prices are quoted in tons.
☐ 3 That's right. They're the standard steaks you'd get in a restaurant, without a bone.
☐ 4 No, not necessarily. The word really just describes a large amount of goods sent together, or the act of sending them.
☐ 5 It's a chain of supermarkets that we sell on to here in Switzerland.
☐ 6 That's right. We want the delivery in August and September.

Focus on ...
missing words

1 Look at these pairs of sentences. Which sentence in each pair is written in note form (N)? Which sentence is in email A (A)?
  1 a Thanks for prompt reply. ☐ ☐
     b Thanks for your prompt reply. ☐ ☐
  2 a Market is coming down slightly. ☐ ☐
     b The market is coming down slightly. ☐ ☐

2 These emails are written in note form because the writers work with each other frequently and this is a way of saving time. Sometimes – but not always – words like *the* and *your* are missing from the emails. Read emails B–E again. Underline the sentences which need an extra word. Insert the words in the emails.

7 Margrit has started a list of words and expressions which might be useful to her in commercial correspondence. Add more words to her list.

customers, promotion, quantities, shipment,

B Please advise

1 Margrit is reading through two emails she is just about to send. Tick ✓ what she does in each email and complete the chart.

		Email A	Email B
1	make an apology		
2	make an enquiry		
3	make an urgent request		
4	make an offer		
5	give information		

2 One of the emails is more direct – very clear and straight to the point – than the other. Complete the sentence. Use some of the information in Exercise 1.

Email ... is more direct because the writer is
....

3 Margrit hopes to receive good news in response to her emails. What does she hope they will say?

....
....

4 Read the two responses. <u>Underline</u> the correct words in these sentences.

  a She receives *some good news and some bad news / only good news / only bad news* from Ricardo.

  b She receives *some good news and some bad news / only good news / only bad news* from Fabio.

A

Delete Reply Reply All Forward Print

Re: Visit of Mr. Peter Muller, Mr. Daniel Wermelinger and Mr. Ivo Luratti in August

Dear Ricardo

Our Managing Director Peter Muller is planning a trip to Brazil in August. He will be accompanied by our new Marketing Director Daniel Wermelinger and Ivo Luratti, whom you already know. They would like to visit the Food Incorporated plant on Monday August 3rd or Tuesday August 4th. The purpose of their visit would be to introduce Daniel Wermelinger to you and your staff and to discuss some new specifications with you. Would you and your product manager be available?

Best regards
Margrit

B

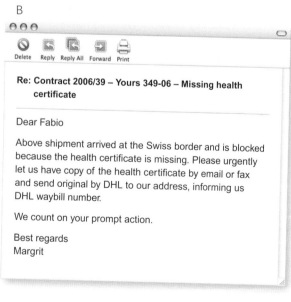

Delete Reply Reply All Forward Print

Re: Contract 2006/39 – Yours 349-06 – Missing health certificate

Dear Fabio

Above shipment arrived at the Swiss border and is blocked because the health certificate is missing. Please urgently let us have copy of the health certificate by email or fax and send original by DHL to our address, informing us DHL waybill number.

We count on your prompt action.

Best regards
Margrit

C

Dear Margrit

I will be on a business trip until August 3rd, I'm afraid. I would like to welcome Messrs Muller, Wermelinger and Luratti to Lins either on Wednesday August 5th or Thursday August 6th. We could have a tour in the manufacturing room with our new cutting and packing line and if there is time I would like to show them also our feedlot. I also would appreciate it if we could have dinner together.

Please advise whether August 5th or 6th are convenient.

Best regards
Ricardo

D

Re: Contract 2006/39 – Yours 349-06 – Missing health certificate

▶ 🖉 1 attachment

Dear Margrit

Attached please find copy of health certificate 345599 668 0034. Original was sent today by DHL 349 3330 334 3333.

Sorry for any inconvenience.

Fabio

5 Read the two responses again. Tick ✓ what the writers do and complete the chart.

	Email C	Email D
1 make an apology		
2 make an enquiry		
3 make an urgent request		
4 make an offer		
5 give information		

6 (Circle) the correct letter in this sentence.

Email *C / D* needs a further reply from Margrit.

7 Read the rest of the correspondence (emails E and F). Make notes of all the arrangements for the visit to Food Incorporated in Lins by completing the diary entries.

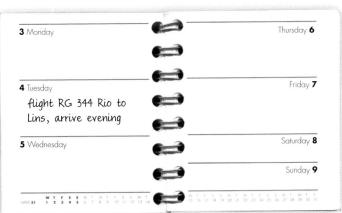

3 Monday / Thursday **6**

4 Tuesday
flight RG 344 Rio to
Lins, arrive evening

Friday **7**

5 Wednesday

Saturday **8**

Sunday **9**

E

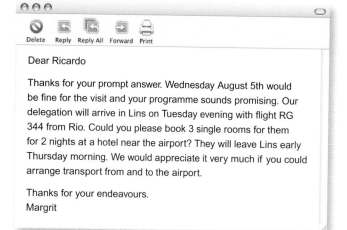

Delete Reply Reply All Forward Print

Dear Ricardo

Thanks for your prompt answer. Wednesday August 5th would be fine for the visit and your programme sounds promising. Our delegation will arrive in Lins on Tuesday evening with flight RG 344 from Rio. Could you please book 3 single rooms for them for 2 nights at a hotel near the airport? They will leave Lins early Thursday morning. We would appreciate it very much if you could arrange transport from and to the airport.

Thanks for your endeavours.
Margrit

F

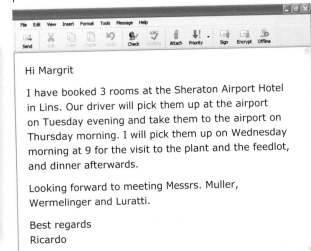

File Edit View Insert Format Tools Message Help

Send Cut Copy Paste Undo Check Spelling Attach Priority Sign Encrypt Offline

Hi Margrit

I have booked 3 rooms at the Sheraton Airport Hotel in Lins. Our driver will pick them up at the airport on Tuesday evening and take them to the airport on Thursday morning. I will pick them up on Wednesday morning at 9 for the visit to the plant and the feedlot, and dinner afterwards.

Looking forward to meeting Messrs. Muller, Wermelinger and Luratti.

Best regards
Ricardo

Class bonus

Is there anything in the correspondence that is unclear? Make a list of questions or things you'd like to check. Work with your classmates. Can anyone help you with the answers to your questions?

E✗tra practice

Ask a friend who uses English at work if you can have a look at some of the things he/she has to read. Ask your friend for clarification of anything you don't understand.

Can-do checklist

Tick what you can do.

	Can do	Need more practice
I can understand general business correspondence.	✓	✓
I can identify new terms in a text and ask for clarification.		
I can identify the purpose of an email in a business context.		

Unit 8
I've got an interview

Get ready to read

● How should you prepare yourself for an interview? Which of these points do you think are important? Tick ✓ one or more of the boxes.
Decide what you're going to wear. ☐
Find out about the organization – its products and services, its customers, its owners, etc. ☐
Prepare a list of questions about the job itself and the organization. ☐
Find out how to get to the place where the interview will be held. ☐
Think about the questions you're likely to be asked. ☐

● What other things should you do before an interview?

go to Useful language p. 84

A Make your first impression count

1 You have been in touch with an employment agency because you need help in finding a new job. Two weeks later you get an email from your recruitment consultant. Read the first two sentences of the email. How do you feel?

> I am delighted to inform you that I have arranged an interview for you at Moody Infrastructure Services Ltd on Thursday 19th October at 5.00 pm.
>
> The interview will be conducted by Mrs Nicola Bootle, Personnel Manager at the address below.

Learning tip

Before you start reading a text in English, ask yourself what you already know about the topic of the text – or what you would do in the situation that it describes. Focusing your thoughts will help you to predict the content of the text and allow you to relate what you read to your own ideas and experiences.

2 Your recruitment consultant has given you a leaflet about interviews. One section has the title *Make your first impression count*. How can you make your first impression count? Write down three ways.

----

3 Now read the section *Make your first impression count* on the opposite page and find out if it mentions any of the three points you wrote down in Exercise 2.

4 There are four paragraphs in this part of the leaflet. Read each paragraph and identify the topic of the paragraph. Then decide upon a heading which summarizes each paragraph.

1 ---
2 ---
3 ---
4 ---

5 Read what four people said about their interview experiences. Now that you have read the leaflet, do you think they did the right thing? Write Y (yes) or N (no).

a My interview was at three o'clock. I arrived a bit early, so I just waited outside and then went into the building at exactly three o'clock. ......

b I came straight from work at the sports centre, so I was wearing my track suit. ......

c I never shake anyone's hand, so I didn't do so at the interview. ......

d I was ten minutes late. I could have phoned the interviewer, but I decided that would take too long. ......

Make your first impression count

1 Your CV has already paved the way and inspired the interviewer to meet you in person. Every element of your arrival for an interview should be detailed. Before you leave home, make sure you know exactly where you have to go. Give yourself enough time to arrive and do a final pre-interview check – a casual attitude to timekeeping is one of the most frequently mentioned negatives by interviewers. If you're going to be late, ensure your consultant is aware so he or she can let the client know.

2 Make sure you know the exact name and title of the person you're meeting. On arrival, take the opportunity to absorb the general atmosphere – do the people in reception seem relaxed? How do they dress? Is there an average profile of staff passing through? You should already have found out as much as you can about the company, but you can read any in-house magazines, brochures or corporate communications and take these with you if allowed. Many interviewers will specifically check back with their reception staff about your general conduct whilst waiting; if you have time, engage the receptionist in some open questions about the company – he or she often has years of experience and will be only too happy to chat.

3 Smart dress is of course a prerequisite. Suits, for both men and women, are the best bet. If you have doubts, play safe and choose the conservative option.

4 It may seem obvious, but remember to smile. Particularly on meeting the interviewer, this is the best ice-breaker. And don't forget to shake hands – both when you arrive and when you leave. If you're offered tea, coffee or water, then do accept if you would like some – this is a good way of relaxing.

6 Read the next section of the leaflet on the right. There are four paragraphs. How many topics are discussed? What are the topics?

----

7 Read the last paragraph again. <u>Underline</u> five pieces of advice.

8 What tips about interviews have you picked up from the texts above?

Focus on ...
related words

1 <u>Underline</u> the words in the first column of the chart in the two texts. What part of speech (noun, verb, etc.) are the words? Write an abbreviation.

word in texts	related words
interview n	interviewer n
arrive	
sure	
reception	
communicate	
mean	

2 Find another related word to the word in the first column in the texts. What part of speech is this word? Complete the second column of the chart.

Interview technique: put preparation to use

1 When communicating, particularly with someone you've just met for the first time, studies show that non-verbal communication counts for over 90% of our actual communication – this includes vocal tones, facial expressions, foot movements, hand and arm gestures, and overall posture. A combination of all of these elements creates the first impression that counts for so much.

2 Your non-verbal communication will say more than your verbal communication – and can even reveal what you actually really mean. When under pressure, candidates often clam up – crossed legs and folded arms indicate defensiveness, negative postures. Eyes also communicate – open, same-level, direct eye contact indicates confidence, whereas looking down and avoiding eye contact suggests insecurity.

3 Strong non-verbal communication when backed with strong verbal communication equals a highly positive interview style.

4 Speak with authority and confidence, but never arrogance. Be aware of your voice speed, volume and pitch – take deep breaths and be calm, measured and assured. Like any situation involving an element of negotiation, don't attempt to speak first unless necessary, and don't fill empty silences with meaningless words and phrases. Also, try not to use filler phrases, e.g. 'You know what I mean' or 'I guess' – these phrases are ambiguous and lack conviction.

B Tell me about yourself

1 Which of these questions might you be asked at a job interview? Tick ✓ the boxes.

a What have been your achievements to date? ☐
b Are you happy with your career to date? ☐
c What do you like about your present job? ☐
d What are your weaknesses? ☐
e What kind of decision do you find most difficult? ☐

2 How would you answer the questions in Exercise 1?

3 Scan the advice from the interview guidance leaflet below. Which of the questions in Exercise 1 are mentioned?

Responding to questions: inspiring confidence

Many questions can be anticipated in advance and it's wise to have some well-constructed answers that you can tailor more closely on the day. It's sensible to have a number of key phrases to use. Remember to always try and make your answers positive.

Q1: Tell me about yourself. (The interviewer is really saying "I want to hear you talk.")
A1: This is just to get things started, but it is a very common question. Write a script, and rehearse it so that it sounds impromptu. Spend a maximum of four minutes describing your qualifications, career history and your range of skills. Emphasise those skills that are relevant to the job on offer.

Q2: What have been your achievements to date? (The interviewer is saying "Are you an achiever?")
A2: Again, this is a common question, so be prepared. Select an achievement that is experience-related and fairly recent. Identify skills you used in this achievement and say what the results were.

Q3: What do you like about your present job? (The interviewer is really trying to find out whether you will enjoy the things the new job has to offer.)
A3: This is a straightforward question. All you have to make sure is that your 'likes' correspond to the skills etc. required for the job on offer. Be positive, describe your job as interesting and diverse, but do not overdo it. After all, you are leaving!

Q4: What do you dislike about your current job? (The interviewer is trying to find out whether the job on offer has responsibilities you will dislike or which will make you unsuitable.)
A4: Be careful with this one! Do not be too specific as you may draw attention to weaknesses, which will leave you open to further problems. One approach is to choose a characteristic of your present company, such as its size, its slow decision-making etc. Give your answer with the air of someone who takes problems and frustrations in your stride as part of the job!

Q5: What are your strengths? (The interviewer simply wants a straightforward answer as to what you are good at.)
A5: This is the one question that you are definitely going to get, so there is no excuse for being unprepared. Concentrate on discussing your main strengths. List three or four explanations of how they could benefit the employer. Strengths to consider include technical proficiency; ability to learn quickly; determination to succeed; positive attitude; your ability to relate to people and achieve a common goal. You may be asked to give examples of the above, so be prepared.

Q6: Tell me about the most difficult situation you've had to face and how you tackled it. (The interviewer is really trying to find out your definition of 'difficult' and whether you can show a logical approach to problem solving using your initiative.)
A6: This can be a trap! To avoid it, select a difficult work situation that was not caused by you and which can be quickly explained in a few sentences. Explain how you defined the problem, what the options were, why you selected the one you did and what the outcome was. Always end on a positive note.

Q7: Why do you want to leave your current employer? (The interviewer is trying to understand and evaluate your motives for moving.)
A7: This should be straightforward. State how you are looking for more challenge, responsibility, experience and a change of environment. NEVER be negative in your reasons for leaving, and it will rarely be appropriate to state salary as the primary motivator.

4 Read the advice again. Match each question in the text with one of these statements. Write the numbers in the boxes.

a Interviewers usually ask this question. [1] ☐ ☐

b This question shouldn't cause you too many problems. ☐ ☐

c This is a difficult question to answer. ☐ ☐

5 Find the words *Be careful with this one!* and *This can be a trap!* Candidates are given strong warnings in these answers. What are they being warned not to do? Tick ✓ one of the boxes.

a They should not describe a situation which might draw attention to their weaknesses. ☐

b They should not describe a situation which had a positive outcome. ☐

c They should not describe a situation which is easy to explain. ☐

6 Read all the advice again more carefully. Do you agree with the advice?

7 Do you want to change your answers to Exercise 2?

Did you know ...?

There are eight parts of speech in the English language. Each word is one of the following: noun, verb, adjective, adverb, article, pronoun, preposition, conjunction.

article   noun adverb verb   adjective
   ↓   ↓   ↓   ↓   ↓
The interviewer simply wants a straightforward answer as to what you are good at.
   ↑   ↑   ↑
conjunction pronoun   preposition

Word families are nouns, verbs, adjectives and adverbs which have the same root. For example: *move, moving, movement, removal, remover, mover* (nouns); *move, remove* (verbs); *movable, unmoved, moving* (adjectives); *movingly* (adverb).

Class bonus

Work in pairs or small groups. Take turns to interview each other for a job. How good an applicant is your partner?

E✗tra practice

Go to www.jobcentreplus.gov.uk. Click on Customers Home and then click on Job Hunting Help. Choose the webpage Interview Preparation. Find some information/ advice on the webpage which is not mentioned in this unit.

Can-do checklist

Tick what you can do.

	Can do	Need more practice
I can relate my own experiences to what I read in a text.		
I can read an interview guidance pack and prepare for an interview.		
I can understand questions I will be asked and the reasoning behind them.		

Unit 9
What's your new job like?

Get ready to read

Get ready to read

○ Circle the words in the sentences so that they are true for your country.

People usually get *less / more* than 20 days' holiday each year.

You get *extra / no extra* days' holiday the longer you work at a place.

In my country there are *more / fewer* than 10 public holidays each year.

People usually get paid once a *week / month*.

They *get / don't get* an extra payment at the end of the year.

○ Here are three job titles which are found in many workplaces. Match them with their definitions.

a   trade union
    representative ☐
b   personnel officer ☐
c   line manager ☐

1   someone who is responsible for managing someone else in a company or business
2   someone who works for the department of a company that deals with its employees when they first join, when they need training or when they have any problems
3   someone who speaks on behalf of members of an organization that protects the rights of people who work in a particular industry

go to Useful language p. 85

A Annual holidays

1 **Yoshima has got a new job at a company called Jackson & Brown Ltd. She is looking at her terms and conditions. Skim the text. What is it about? Tick ✓ the correct box.**

a   how many days' holiday she will get ☐
b   when she can take her holidays ☐
c   payment if she doesn't take her holidays ☐

Learning tip

We use neutral language in most of our everyday communication. However, sometimes we have to read texts written in formal language – legal documents, in particular. The language is often impersonal: the third person and the passive are used; there are no contractions; sentences are long and complicated; and there are lots of nouns and noun phrases. Formal language is unlike the spoken language that we are used to. You can make sure you have understood a formal text by putting it into less formal everyday language. This means rephrasing the sentences rather than simply replacing individual words with less formal alternatives.

2 **Yoshima has asked a colleague to explain to her how much holiday she will get. Read the introductory section of the *Terms and Conditions* more carefully and look at the chart. Match the beginnings and endings of her colleague's explanations. Write the numbers in the boxes.**

a   For your first five years, ☐
b   March 31st is an important date ☐
c   The number of days' holiday you get in your first year depends on ☐
d   You need to start work on the 1st of the month ☐
e   If you start work on February 1st, ☐
f   However, if you start on February 15th for example, ☐

1   to get holiday for that month.
2   you'll only have worked one full month so you'll get two days' holiday.
3   you'll have worked two full months by the end of the financial year.
4   you'll get 22 days' holiday a year.
5   how many complete months you have worked by March 31st.
6   because it's the end of the financial year.

3 Yoshima actually started work at Jackson & Brown Ltd on May 8th. Complete this sentence.

She will get .... days' holiday before March 31st.

TERMS AND CONDITIONS

Annual holidays

The table below gives details of holiday entitlement from the start of employment until the end of the financial year (31 March). Holiday entitlement rises from 22 days per annum to 25 days per annum after 5 years' continuous service at 31 March.

For the purpose of calculating holiday entitlement, month of service means any calendar month throughout which the person has been in the employment of the company.

Qualifying period	Holiday entitlement
12 months of service complete	22 days
11 months, but less than 12	21 days
10 months, but less than 11	19 days
9 months, but less than 10	17 days
8 months, but less than 9	15 days
7 months, but less than 8	13 days
6 months, but less than 7	11 days
5 months, but less than 6	9 days
4 months, but less than 5	7 days
3 months, but less than 4	6 days
2 months, but less than 3	4 days
1 month, but less than 2	2 days

1 Any person who leaves the service of the company after a period of employment in respect of which he/she has not received a holiday shall be entitled to the annual holidays accruing to him/her or shall receive the payment which would have been due if the holiday were taken at the time of leaving.

2 No employee shall be entitled to annual holidays exceeding five weeks excepting in such circumstances where by mutual agreement up to 5 days' annual leave may be carried forward into a new leave year.

3 Employees are entitled to eight statutory days holiday plus a floating day over the Christmas / New Year period. Should an employee be required to work on one of these public holidays, he/she will be entitled to equivalent time off in lieu to be taken at a mutually agreed time.

Did you know ...?

Public holidays in Britain are called Bank Holidays. An Act of Parliament in 1871 required the Bank of England and other banks to close on specific days of the year. These days became public holidays; they are sometimes referred to as 'statutory' days' holiday, i.e. they are controlled by law. If a bank holiday falls on a Saturday or Sunday, the next working day becomes the holiday. Bank holidays in Britain are:

New Year's Day (January 1)
Good Friday and Easter Monday (the dates change every year)
First Monday in May
Spring Bank Holiday (last Monday in May)
Summer Bank Holiday (last Monday in August)
Christmas Day (December 25)
Boxing Day (December 26)

4 Imagine you are Yoshima's colleague. Use the information in the rest of the text to answer her questions. Remember to rephrase the text in less formal language. The dictionary definitions below the questions may help you.

a What happens if you decide to leave the company and you haven't taken all your days' holiday?

----

b What happens if you don't use all your days' holiday before the end of the financial year?

----

c Do you get any extra days' holiday at Christmas and New Year?

----

d What happens if you have to work on a public holiday?

----

accrue /əˈkruː/ *verb* [I] FORMAL to increase in number or amount over a period of time: *Interest will accrue* **on the** *account at a rate of 7%.* ○ *Little benefit will accrue* **to** *London* (= London will receive little benefit) *from the new road scheme.*

excepting /ɪkˈsep.tɪŋ/ *prep, conjunction* FORMAL not including: *All the people who were on the aircraft have now been identified, excepting one.*

● **in respect of** *sth* (ALSO **with respect to** *sth*) FORMAL in connection with something: *I am writing with respect to your letter of 15 June.*

lieu /ljuː/ ⑤ /luː/ *noun* FORMAL **in lieu (of)** instead (of): *The paintings were left to the nation by the Duke of Norfolk in lieu of inheritance taxes.*

Class bonus

Work with a partner. Ask and answer the questions in Exercise 4 about your own workplace. Choose an imaginary job if you don't work yourself.

B Changes to pay cycle

1 You are now going to read a letter which is about *Changes to pay cycle*. Look at these dictionary definitions of *cycle*. What do you think *Changes to pay cycle* might mean?

2 Three weeks after Yoshima started work at Jackson & Brown Ltd, she received this letter. Answer these questions.

   a Who is the letter from?
   b Who is the letter to – to Yoshima only, or to a group of people?

> **cycle** BICYCLE ❶ /ˈsaɪ.kl̩/ *noun* [C] a bicycle
> **cycle** /ˈsaɪ.kl̩/ *verb* [I] to ride a bicycle **cycling** /ˈsaɪ.klɪŋ/ *noun* [U]: *We did a lot of cycling in France last year.*
> **cyclist** /ˈsaɪ.klɪst/ *noun* [C] someone who rides a bicycle
> **cycle** SERIES /ˈsaɪ.kl̩/ *noun* [C] **1** a group of events which happen in a particular order, one following the other, and which are often repeated: *the life cycle of a moth* **2** one in a series of movements that a machine performs: *the spin cycle* **cyclical** /ˈsaɪ.klɪ.kəl/ /ˈsɪk.lɪ-/ *adj* (ALSO **cyclic**) *Changes in the economy have followed a cyclical pattern.*
> **cycle** PLAYS/POEMS /ˈsaɪ.kl̩/ *group noun* [C] a group of plays, poems, etc. written by one person and connected with each other by dealing with the same characters or ideas: *It's one in a cycle of plays that are being performed on successive evenings.*

J&B Jackson & Brown Ltd

Head Office, Bradford House,
234 Manningham Road Bolton BL3 5QS
t: 01204 249241 f: 01204 790061

1 June 20_

Dear Colleague

Re: Changes to pay cycle

1 I am writing to make you aware of some forthcoming changes to the payment dates for your salary. During the past few weeks, we have been discussing with your trade union representatives our intention to change the frequency of the payment of your salary from monthly to every four weeks. The reason for this change is to enable us to improve the efficiency of the payroll system and to make it easier for you to understand what you have been paid.

2 On Thursday 30 August you will be paid your monthly basic pay up to and including 31 August. The last Thursday in the month is the normal monthly pay day. On 13 September you will be paid basic pay up to and including 14 September. You will then be paid again 4 weeks later on 11 October, for time up to 12 October. The timetable of 4-weekly payments for the remainder of the financial year is listed below:

8 November	31 January
6 December	28 February
3 January 20__	28 March

3 I understand that the transfer to a four-weekly pay cycle may cause some of you disruption to your monthly pay routines, for example mortgage or rent repayments. In recognition of this initial disturbance and to assist you through this time, we are offering a loan facility for a maximum of three weeks' wages (net pay), for those who may find it difficult to budget for this change. I have enclosed a form detailing this loan. Please ensure you complete and return the form by 30 June if you wish to take advantage of this offer. If you choose to use the loan facility, this will be paid on 13 September.

4 Of course, should you wish to discuss the contents of this letter, your line manager will have further information. If you still have any concerns or you have a personal query you wish to discuss, then from 13 June until 1 July you can call the following number: 01204 249259.

5 I hope that this letter clarifies the changes for you and would like to take this opportunity to thank you in advance for your co-operation. Further information to explain how your new payslip will look will be available over the coming months.

Yours sincerely
Tina Grey
Group General Manager, Personnel Services

3 Skim the letter. Which paragraphs contain the answers to these questions? Write the paragraph numbers in the boxes.

a (What are the changes?) ☐

b (What are the reasons for the changes?) ☐

c (When will the changes start?) ☐

d (How will the cycle continue?) ☐

e (What problems might employees have with this new pay cycle?) ☐

f (What is the company offering to do about this problem?) ☐

g (What exactly do employees have to do if they want to benefit from this offer?) ☐

h (When will they benefit from the offer?) ☐

i (What should employees do if they have a question about the changes to the pay cycle?) ☐

4 Read the letter more carefully. Answer the questions in Exercise 3.

5 Imagine you worked at Jackson & Brown Ltd. How would you feel about the pay changes mentioned in this letter?

Focus on ...
compound nouns

1 *Pay cycle* is a compound noun – a word that combines two different words. Find other examples of compound nouns with *pay* in the letter. Note that some are one word and some are two, and that sometimes *pay* is the first word and sometimes it is the second word.) Write a list.

payroll ....

2 Complete these sentences with the compound nouns you found in the letter.
   a The four-weekly .... will be less than the monthly one.
   b There is no overtime at Jackson & Brown Ltd – you only get ....
   c The new .... will still be a Thursday.
   d Your .... on September 13th will look different from the others.
   e Tax has to be deducted from your salary, so your .... is always less than the figure they tell you.
   f Some people don't have particular .... – they pay everything by direct debit.

3 Consult an Advanced Learner's Dictionary (such as the *Cambridge Advanced Learner's Dictionary*). How many other compound nouns beginning with *pay* are there? Make a list of those connected with work.
   ....
   ....
   ....
   ....

E✗tra practice

Do you receive letters in English in your workplace? If not, try and have a look at a book of business letters. Find examples of neutral and formal language.

Can-do checklist

Tick what you can do.

	Can do	Need more practice
I can rephrase formal language into more neutral everyday language.	✓	✓
I can understand part of a legal contract about annual holidays.		
I can understand a letter about pay cycles.		

Unit 10
I've got Thursday off

Get ready to **read**

- Complete these sentences about office workers in your country with numbers.
  Most office workers start work at _____ .
  They finish at _____ .
  Most office workers work _____ hours each week.
  They work _____ days a week.

- Imagine you've got a dentist's appointment for 4.30pm on Thursday afternoon. You usually finish work at 5.00pm and it will take you half an hour to get to the surgery. Which of these things are you most likely to say to your boss and which are you least likely to say? (1 = most likely, 5 = least likely)
  Can I have Thursday off? I haven't used all my holiday yet. ☐
  Can I have Thursday afternoon off? I've got half a day holiday left. ☐
  Can I leave early on Thursday afternoon? I worked late one day last week. ☐
  Can I work through my lunch hour on Thursday? I need to leave early. ☐
  Can I leave at four o'clock on Thursday? I'll come in an hour early on Friday. ☐

go to Useful language p. 85

A I'd like to work flexitime

1 **Jana is writing an email to her friend Katya about her new job. Read part of the email below. Answer the questions.**

a What problems has Jana had – and has she got?
b What do you think she should do about the problems?

Everybody is very nice. We work 37½ hours a week. I start at 8.30 am, have an hour for lunch (anytime between 12 and 2 pm) and finish work at 5 pm. I was late for work three times last week because of the rush-hour traffic and I don't think my boss was very pleased! I've got to go to the dentist at 4.30 on Thursday afternoon and I haven't got round to asking her if I can leave early. Some people would just take the day off, of course – but I wouldn't get paid. What would you do?

---

2 **Some of Jana's colleagues are talking about flexitime. One of them shows her a webpage on the Internet. Read the first two sections of the webpage and find out what flexitime is. Complete this definition with no more than 20 words.**

Flexitime is a system of working in which people _____

---

3 **As well as** *flexitime,* (circle) **other words in the text beginning with the letters** *flexi.*

4 **With flexitime, you set up a time** *bank.* **Answer these questions.**

a Which other words from the topic of banking are mentioned in the text?
---
b How does flexitime work similarly to and differently from a bank account?
---

5 **Look at the third section. Which of the problems mentioned in Jana's email are addressed here?**

6 **Look at the fourth section. How are the problems mentioned in Jana's email addressed here?** Underline **the solutions in the webpage.**

www.borer.co.uk/pges/case_studies/flexitime

borer DATA SYSTEMS

Flexitime

1 **Flexitime helps to maintain a work-life balance**

Flexitime is a scheme where an organisation offers its employees the opportunity of a flexible working hours arrangement.

2 **How does flexitime work?**

Essentially, your organisation will agree standard or core hours that must be worked by employees as well as flexible working hours where employees can come and go as they please. For example, you might agree to:

- Arrive for work between 0730–1000 (flexitime)
- Guarantee to be there between 1000–1200 (core time)
- Take your lunch break between 1200–1400 (flexible lunch hour)
- Guarantee to be there from 1400–1600 (core time)
- Leave between 1600–1930 (flexitime)

The hours you work between these times are credited to you. In effect, you set up a time bank with your employer. An employee is obliged to work the basic core hours and has the flexibility to clock in/out during the other hours.

Most schemes allow you a credit or debit margin, often of about 10 hours. For example, if you work a 35-hour week, then over four weeks, you will 'owe' your employer 140 hours. These four weeks are your 'accounting period'; if you work more than 140 hours in four weeks then you will be in credit, and if you work fewer hours then you will owe time to your employer. If you go beyond your credit margin, into surplus, you may have to give up your extra hours; if you go beyond your debit margin, into debt, you may be disciplined or lose pay.

One of the best-liked features of flexitime is flexileave. You can turn your credit hours into time off. Depending on the scheme you are in, this might be one or two half days a month or one full day, or you may be able to add days to your holiday entitlement.

3 **What are the advantages for employees?**

- Allows you to schedule your travel time to avoid congestion
- Allows you bank time to be used for leisure/personal activities
- Personal matters can be sorted without having to take time off
- Parents can schedule their day to pick up young children
- Reduces absenteeism
- Reduces stress and fatigue and unfocused employees
- Increases morale
- Increases employee satisfaction and production

4 **What are the advantages for employers?**

- A benefit to retain and attract new employees
- Work time visits to doctor/dentist are in employee's time
- Measures employee's attendance – you only pay for time in attendance. Late arrival caused by traffic congestion, delayed trains, etc. is at employee's expense
- An incentive to complete tasks instead of being carried forward to the next day as extra hours worked count towards the final target

---

7 Look at the last two sections again. Which of the advantages for employees do you think could also be included in the section about advantages for employers? Tick ✓ one of the boxes.

a none of them ☐
b the first four ☐
c the last four ☐
d all of them ☐

8 The webpage mentions the advantages of flexitime. Can you think of any disadvantages to either the employee or the employer?

9 Would you like to work flexitime? Why? / Why not?

Focus on ...
phrasal verbs

1 Scan the text and find these phrasal verbs. Match them with their meanings on the right.

a set up   collect
b give up   lose
c pick up   start

2 Replace the verbs in these sentences with phrasal verbs. Use the verbs in the box + *up*.

> bring   do   fix   give   split   turn

a She <u>arrived</u> at my house late one night. ___turned up___
b I'd like to <u>arrange</u> a meeting with you next week. _____
c I've <u>stopped</u> trying to help her. _____
d Why won't this zip <u>fasten</u>? _____
e Sue and her boyfriend <u>separated</u> last week. _____
f The boys were <u>raised</u> by their grandmother. _____

Did you know ...?

Of all the words in the English language, the word *set* has the most definitions.

B Up-to-date staffing information

1 Jana and her colleagues decide to talk to their boss about the possibility of introducing flexitime. They are discussing what to say to him and what he might ask them. How do you think they should answer these questions?

a What are the advantages of flexitime to me? ....

b What are the drawbacks? ....

c How will flexitime work in practice? ....

d Could the system be abused? ....

2 The webpage they have been looking at is part of the website www.borer.co.uk Here is part of another webpage from this website. Skim the text. What is the main purpose of this webpage? Tick ✓ one of the boxes.

a to give information ☐

b to explain how to use a website ☐

c to sell a product ☐

3 Read the webpage again. Are these sentences true (T) or false (F)?

a The word *you* is used a lot. ......

b Phrasal verbs are used. ......

c Lots of relatively short words are used. ......

d The active form is used more than the passive form. ......

Learning tip

When the register of a text is impersonal and technical, long words are more commonly used. Nouns are often used together in groups, with one noun describing another noun. (The noun *holiday* describes the noun *pay* in *holiday pay*, for example.) You will need to be able to recognize such groups and to work out which is the main noun within the group (it is usually the last one). This will help you to understand the structure of the sentence and the text.

---

www.borer.co.uk/atracswebmanagement

borer DATA SYSTEMS

Enterprise Class
Facilities Information system

1 ATRACS Web Enabled Attendance Management

Attendance management systems require considerable and sustained administrative effort to effectively produce meaningful management information. Effort is required to distribute reports and summaries, adjust attendance records for absences, missed clockings and holidays, or answer staff queries. Implementing an automated time and attendance system makes things very easy for both employees and their managers alike.

2 Management Information and Control

ATRACS Web puts the information directly onto the manager's desktop by linking attendance data held on the ATRACS database to an Intranet Web Site. Then by simply using the web browser supplied with every PC, managers can instantly:

Review employee absence history

View employee attendance record

List all staff in attendance

Correct employee attendance record to accommodate absence or a missed clocking

Authorise adjustments requested by employees

3 Managers with password clearance can use a web browser to check manning levels, review staff attendance and locate staff. Web enabling provides:

Up-to-date staffing information so that managers can, at a click, see who is in attendance, on holiday, sick leave or absent

Less administration manager can review attendance data from their desktop PCs

Reduced paperwork attendance reports are distributed electronically to managers

Efficient handling of queries members of staff can review their own attendance record without having to refer to a manager

4 Confidentiality and Security

All data is password protected with individual passwords for staff and managers. Staff may browse their own individual attendance records while managers can view the attendance details for only their own workgroups. Before data can be accessed via the Web, members of staff must first be identified by entry of user ID and personal password.

To arrange a demo of the Flexitime system, or for further enquiries
web@borer.co.uk

4 Here are four compound nouns (in *italics*) from the first section. Which is the main noun in the group? Look at the questions if you need some help.

a *Attendance management systems* – What require(s) considerable and sustained administrative effort – attendance, management or systems?

b *management information* – Is this in order to produce meaningful management or meaningful information?

c *attendance records* – Is effort required to adjust attendance or to adjust records?

d *staff queries* – Does implementing attendance or implementing a system make things easy?

e *attendance system* – Is implementing attendance or implementing a system easy?

5 Complete these compound nouns from the second section. Circle the more/most important noun. Then find other noun groups in the last two sections. Circle the more/most important noun.

a management ....

b attendance ....

c web ....

d employee absence ....

e employee attendance ....

6 From your reading of the webpage, how do you think **ATRACS Web Enabled Attendance Management** works?

7 Look at another part of the same webpage. What information does this give about how the ATRACS system works?

Name	Target	Credit	Balance	In	Out	Attendance	
Asling C J D	37:30	38:19	0:49	8.09 13:12	12.20 16:59	7:58	Standard Day
Davies Ms H A	37:30	38:09	0:39	8:14	12:03K	3:49 3:45	Standard ½ Flexi
Heeley H S	37:30	41:41	4:41	8:00 13:05	12:04 18:04	9:03	
Parker T C	37:30	37.21	-0:09	8:03 13:09	12:17 16:00	7:05	Standard Day

8 Imagine you are Jana. What would you tell your boss about ATRACS? Decide what you would say.

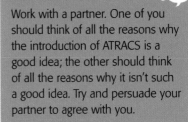

Class bonus

Work with a partner. One of you should think of all the reasons why the introduction of ATRACS is a good idea; the other should think of all the reasons why it isn't such a good idea. Try and persuade your partner to agree with you.

9 How would you feel if flexitime was introduced into your company?

E X tra practice

Further information about ATRACS is available on the Borer website.

Can-do checklist

Tick what you can do.

	Can do	Need more practice
I can understand the benefits of working flexitime.	✓	✓
I can understand a description of a system which monitors staff attendance.		
I can identify the most important noun in a group of nouns.		

Get ready to read

- The words in the box are types of business correspondence. Match the words with their definitions.

  | agenda   memo   minutes   report |

  a .... message or other information in writing sent by one person to another in the same business organization
  b .... description of an event or situation
  c .... list of matters to be discussed at a meeting
  d .... written record of what was said at a meeting

- Have you ever read any of the types of business correspondence above?

go to Useful language p. 85

- Tick ✓ the sentences that are true for you.
  I never go to meetings. ☐
  I go to a meeting about once a week. ☐
  I have one or more meetings every day. ☐
  I seem to spend all my time in meetings. ☐

- Who do you meet with? Tick ✓ the boxes.
  your colleagues ☐
  your boss ☐
  visitors from other companies ☐

A Colleague Council Meeting

1 **Emma Brown is an accounts administrator and she works in the offices of a large telecommunications company. She has agreed to represent the accounts department on the Colleague Council – a group of staff members which discusses problems in the workplace. She has just received this memo. What is it about? Tick ✓ the correct sentence.**

  a The memo is in connection with a meeting that has taken place. ☐
  b The memo is in connection with a meeting that will take place. ☐

Did you know ...?

Ref, in this memo, is a written abbreviation for 'Reference'. Other abbreviations which are used in correspondence include *p* for 'page' – and *pp* for 'pages' – and *cont* or *contd*, which is used at the bottom of a page to show that the letter, report, etc. is not finished and continues overleaf.
Note that *Re* (in the memo) is not an abbreviation. It is simply used to mean 'on the subject of'.

Memo

To: Colleague Council Member
From: Jane Simmons/Liz Bateman
Ref: 16008–1
Date: 16.10.20__
Re: Colleague Council Minutes

Enclosed is a copy of the Minutes from the recent Council Meeting.
Please make sure you feed back on any specific issues to those colleagues who raised them and that you file the Minutes for future reference.
A schedule of meeting dates for next year will be forwarded to you under separate cover.
Looking forward to meeting with you again soon.

Regards
Jane & Liz

2 Did Emma attend the meeting? Scan the minutes and find the answer.

Colleague Council Meeting <u>3rd Oct 20</u>

Chairperson: Jane Simmons
Minutes Secretary: Liz Bateman
NB – Blue font indicates most recent response

1 **Welcome**

Jane Simmons welcomed all colleagues to the meeting. She explained the aim of the Colleague Council – issues which are of concern to staff members can be raised and discussed by the group, and then addressed to Personnel Manager, Penny Kacelnik, in the second half of the meeting. Meetings will be held four times a year.

MATTERS ARISING FROM THE MINUTES

2 **Lifting of international call barring**

The council asked if it would be possible to have the phone system changed so that international calls can be made.
All phones in Sales & Marketing will be modified in November to allow for international calls. Anyone else who needs to call overseas should contact Asif Din in IT.

3 **Recycling of paper**

The council enquired if the correct route for raising recycling issues was through John Evans, Office Services Manager.
Penny agreed that this was the correct route. She also added that she would welcome everyone looking at the paper they generate and cutting down if possible. Individuals are reminded that they can also make a difference by turning lights and monitors etc off.

4 **Healthy snack options in vending machines**

The council requested that a healthy range of snacks be available from the snack machine.
Penny reminded everyone that the canteen offers healthy lunch-time options. She will discuss the contents of the machine with the leasers when the lease comes up for renewal next month. Feedback to be given at Jan meeting.

5 **Expenses policy for business trips**

The council asked for clarification of the expenses policy. Two issues were raised: the timeframe for claiming expenses, and business insurance for use of own cars.
Penny explained that claims should be made within 10 days of the end of the month. However, if necessary where there is financial hardship or ad-hoc usage, claims can be made weekly. The Company had previously issued information on business insurance – this states that colleagues are normally covered for travelling to and from meetings on their normal insurance polices. This information will be reissued on the intranet, but colleagues must check with their own insurers to ensure that their policy covers them.

6 **Removal of study grants**

The council expressed regret that study grants for non-professional courses were no longer available. People should be encouraged to take language courses, for example, given our growing international market.
Penny explained that Management felt this money could be better used on paying for courses which would lead to professional qualifications, such as Accountancy, Credit Control. A suggestion was made that in-house language courses could be taught by members of staff.
Feasibility of in-house language courses to be researched before next meeting.

Next Meeting: Will be January, precise date to be confirmed
Attendees: Louisa Barlow, Gary Brown, Natalie Cole, Orla Doyle, Tariq Ali, Penny Kacelnik (Personnel Officer)
Apologies: Emma Brown, Parvinder Miskry

3 Emma had received an email from Sam, one of her colleagues, just before the Colleague Council meeting. Read Sam's email. Then skim the minutes of the meeting. Was the issue raised by anyone else?

Three years ago, I did a web design course and I got a grant of £50 towards the cost of the course. This year I wanted to do a Spanish course, but I was told that I wouldn't get any money towards it. I'm sorry money's not available any more because this might mean that some people can't afford to do classes.

4 The Personnel Manager attended part of the Colleague Council Meeting. What was her response to the issue mentioned in the email? Tick ✓ the correct box.

a Money would be available for non-professional courses. ☐
b Money would be available for professional courses. ☐
c Money would be available for in-house language courses. ☐

5 Would you be likely to discuss the same issues at a Colleague Council Meeting in your workplace? What other issues might you raise?

Focus on ...
reported speech

1 Find these words in the minutes:
The council asked, enquired, requested, asked for. <u>Underline</u> the whole sentence in which the words appear. These sentences are all examples of reported speech – they report what someone actually said (their direct speech).

2 How did Colleague Council members actually make the comments above? Rephrase the sentences in direct speech.
a <u>Will it be possible to have the phone system changed so that international calls can be made?</u>
b ....
c ....
d ....

B Here's my report

1 Read this email that Emma sent Sam after she read the minutes of the Colleague Council Meeting. Who is going to research the feasibility of setting up an in-house language course?

I wasn't able to attend the recent Colleague Council Meeting, but someone else raised the issue of study grants. It seems that these are no longer available to staff who want to do courses that are not directly connected with their work. However, I understand that Penny Kacelnik has spoken to Alejandro Mendoza about setting up a Spanish course for members of staff. (He's been asked to write a report before the next Colleague Council meeting.) You might be interested in that instead of an evening class.

Emma

---

2 Sam is very interested in doing an in-house Spanish course. Here are the questions he is discussing with Emma. What other questions might they discuss? Add these to the list.

a Will we have to buy a book?
b How often will we have a lesson?
c Will Alejandro teach us?
d How do I get a place on the course?
e What exactly will we study?
f Do I need to know some Spanish in order to do the course?
g How much will the course cost?

Learning tip

Always look at the title and headings before you start reading a text. This is because they help you to understand what is and what is not in a text. You will usually find headings in business correspondence – letters, minutes, reports – because the aim is for maximum clarity.

3 Alejandro discusses the report with Emma, and he tells her that the report has the following headings. Where will she find the answers to Sam's questions? Match the questions in Exercise 2 with the headings/topics below as best you can. Write the letters in the boxes.

1 INTRODUCTION ☐   5 TIMING AND LOCATION ☐
2 COURSE CONTENT ☐   6 COURSE MATERIAL ☐
3 ENROLMENT ☐   7 TEACHER ☐
4 LEVEL ☐   8 FOLLOW-UP ☐

Did you know ...?

Spanish is one of six official working languages of the United Nations and one of the most used global languages. It is spoken in most South American countries, as well as in certain parts of Europe, Asia, Africa and Oceania. Spanish is also the second most widely spoken language in the United States and the most popular foreign language for study in US schools and universities. It is estimated that the combined total of native and non-native Spanish speakers is 400–500 million, probably making it the third most spoken language by total number of speakers.

4 Skim Alejandro's report on the opposite page and check your answers to Exercise 3.

5 Read the report more carefully and check the answers to the questions in Exercise 2.

6 Read the report again. There are issues in three of the paragraphs which the Personnel Manager might need to discuss with the Managing Director. Tick ✓ the three paragraphs.

1 ☐   2 ☐   3 ☐   4 ☐
5 ☐   6 ☐   7 ☐   8 ☐

7 What do you think of Alejandro's suggestions? Which ones are good and which would you change? How?

8 Imagine you work in an office environment and have been asked to give a course in your language. What difficulties would you have in setting it up? Consider the questions in Exercise 2.

9 Have you ever studied on an in-house course? What was it like?

LANGUAGE CLASSES REPORT

1 INTRODUCTION
I was asked by the Personnel Manager to investigate the feasibility of organising a course of Spanish language-training for members of staff, and to make recommendations about the implementation of such a course. I have discussed this matter with two of my Spanish-speaking colleagues and we all feel that the company would benefit enormously from this development. We have discussed various aspects of such a course and would like to make the following suggestions.

2 COURSE CONTENT
The focus would be on the business world, rather than a general Spanish course. Our aim would be to prepare participants for dealing with Spanish-speaking visitors, and for dealing with telephone and email queries.

3 ENROLMENT
Places should be available to anyone in the company, but the course will be aimed at staff who need to use Spanish in their jobs. Twelve is an ideal group size, although the number could rise to 16 if there was such a demand.

4 LEVEL
The level of the course will be elementary and students will be either beginners or know only a little Spanish.

5 TIMING AND LOCATION
We propose two lessons per week, of an hour each. Taking into account the fact that the most popular days off during the week are Monday and Friday, we suggest Tuesday and Thursday for the classes. The course could be in lunchtime or after work, although our preference is that it takes place in work time. We feel that this would ensure a higher level of commitment from the participants. A register would be taken at the end of every lesson so that attendance feedback could be given to managers if necessary. The meeting room at the top of the stairs would be ideal since this room already has a whiteboard.

6 COURSE MATERIAL
We would suggest using Level 1 of the business course Negocios. This is divided into 20 short units, and it should be possible to complete a unit's work in a week. Participants can either buy their own copy of the book, or the company could buy a class set. These could then be re-used with further groups. The book is accompanied by a Teacher's Book and a CD, both of which are invaluable. We assume that the Company would purchase these on our behalf.

7 TEACHER
Esteban Hübner, who works in IT, would teach the class. He already has teaching experience, having taught Spanish in Salamanca for the Don Quixote chain of language schools. Esteban would appreciate one hour's preparation time to be built into his working hours every week. If the class(es) were to be given at lunchtime, then he would appreciate the time off in lieu.

8 FOLLOW-UP
If an initial course goes ahead, then we suggest appraising its success on an ongoing basis. The initial group could go on to a second course (the second half of the book), or if sufficient people were interested, we could repeat the course with a second group.

I look forward to your comments on this report.

Alejandro Mendoza
November 26th 20___

Class bonus

Discuss ways of improving your English – either at work or in your free time. Make a class list of all the things you can do. You will probably get some ideas from your classmates.

E X tra practice

Find out about business English courses on the Internet. Are there any in-house courses on offer in your country?

Can-do checklist

Tick what you can do.

	Can do	Need more practice
I can understand the minutes of a meeting and act upon them.		
I can use headings to predict the content of a report.		
I can understand a report and consider its implications.		

Unit 12
The course is in English

Get ready to read

- If you were to go and study English or study at a university in another country, where would you go? Put these countries in order of preference (1 = favourite, 5 = least favourite).

  Australia ☐
  Canada ☐
  New Zealand ☐
  United Kingdom ☐
  United States ☐

- Here are some reasons students give for going abroad to an English-language university. Which reason would you be most likely to give? Tick ✓ one of the boxes.

  'I had never lived overseas and always wanted to. That's why, when I got the chance, I jumped at it! I wanted a bit of adventure.' ☐

  'I had little choice. My subject, petrochemical engineering, is not very well-developed in my country, so I had to go overseas to study it.' ☐

  'I thought I would get a better job back home if I had a qualification from an American university.' ☐

  'I just fancied a bit of a break. I could do some studying, as well as visit places of interest and do some exciting things.' ☐

  'I thought it would be good to do a business studies course and improve my English at the same time.' ☐

go to Useful language p. 85

A Pre-departure decisions

1 Akihiro has decided that he would like to study at a university overseas. He has just bought a book called *Study Skills for Speakers of English as a Second Language* and is about to start reading it. Tick ✓ the section which is most likely to be first in the book.

   a GETTING ORGANISED ☐
   b YOUR UNIVERSITY STUDIES ☐
   c UNIVERSITY LIFE ☐

Learning tip

Headings, italics and bold indicate what type of information you are going to find in a text. Specific signalling words or phrases, such as *However, Therefore, Furthermore*, can help you to predict what is coming next in the text. When the words are at the beginning of a sentence, they link the new sentence to the previous one. Words and phrases like *because, so, in order to* are usually found in the middle of a sentence (although they can be at the beginning) and they link the two parts of that sentence. Recognizing and understanding such words and phrases can help you to read more efficiently. They also help you to understand the structure of the text.

2 Akihiro is reading the first chapter of the book. It is called *Pre-departure decisions*. Here is the very first paragraph in the book. Read the first paragraph and circle the correct options to complete the text.

Pre-departure decisions

All over the world students are changing countries for their university studies. This chapter is written for people who are at the first stage of planning. They have already decided to go, (1) *but / since / so that / in order to* are still thinking about which country and university would be right for them. Part of the decision depends on which courses are offered at which university. (2) *As a result, / However, / In addition, / Therefore,* some students choose their place of study because they like the country, its language and its culture.

Did you know ...?

At any given time, more than a million international students around the world are studying English in an English-speaking country. The five most popular destinations in order are: USA, Britain, Australia, New Zealand and Canada. The USA attracts the greatest international mix of students. Australia attracts mostly Asian students; just over one-third come from Japan.

3 Here are four short extracts from the first chapter. Match the headings with the extracts below.

Available places   Entry requirements   Reputation
The country

a ----------------------------------
   Some universities have a very good 'name' and are famous around the world.

b ----------------------------------
   The 'entry requirements' are the grades and qualifications you need to take the course of your choice.

c ----------------------------------
   Some students choose a country first and then a university. Maybe a family member has already studied there

d ----------------------------------
   Sometimes it is very difficult to get a place on a particular course, such as Law,

4 What other things should you consider when choosing a university overseas? Think of three more things.

5 How would the extracts in Exercise 3 continue if the next words were the following? Write two sentences / sentence endings for each extract in Exercise 3.

a *Furthermore, their staff are international figures and well-known in the world of research.*

a *However, they may not do the course you want.*

a Furthermore / However
b For example / Therefore
c and / or
d even though / since

6 Scan the text below and compare your sentences in Exercise 5 with the words the authors have written.

7 Read the text again. Which of the reasons given for studying at a particular university are the most important in your opinion?

Pre-departure decisions

All over the world students are changing countries for their university studies. This chapter is written for people who are at the first stage of planning. They have already decided to go, but are still thinking about which country and university would be right for them. Part of the decision depends on which courses are offered at which university. In addition, some students choose their place of study because they like the country, its language and its culture.

> This chapter answers the following questions:
> * How do students choose their university?
> * How can students get scholarships?
> * What tests and examinations measure students' English levels?

▶ **How do students decide where to go?**

Here are the reasons people gave for studying at a particular university.

Reputation
Some universities have a very good 'name' and are famous around the world. However, as well as thinking about the 'name', think about whether the university you have in mind is strong in the subjects you want to study.

The cost
The cost of going to another country includes much more than the university fees. What the cost of living will mean for you and your family depends partly on the rate of exchange between the two countries.

Entry requirements
The 'entry requirements' are the grades and qualifications you need to take the course of your choice. For example, if you want to become a (medical) doctor, some universities want you to prove that you are very good at English and maybe that you have taken subjects like English and History in high school.

The country
Some students choose a country first and then a university. Maybe a family member has already studied there and enjoyed meeting the people and learning about the culture.

Meeting students from your country
Another reason for choosing a particular country is because many people from your country are there. In that case you will be able to speak your own language sometimes and find food that is familiar.

Visas
One big question to think about is how easy it is for someone with your passport to get a visa to study in a particular country.

Available places
Sometimes it is very difficult to get a place on a particular course, such as Law, even though you have all the entry requirements.

Course dates
Year-long courses usually start in September in the Northern Hemisphere and in March in the Southern Hemisphere. However, many courses have a semester system which means you can start any course every six months or even at a Summer School.

The university site
Do you like to live near the city or in a quieter, more peaceful area? If you want to travel to town sometimes, how easy is the transport? Some universities have more than one campus.

B **Why Study Oz?**

1 Akihiro lives in Tokyo and he has just finished his first degree there. He thinks he would like to do a Master's in Australia. Read this section from *Study Skills for Speakers of English as a Second Language*. Which website should he use in order to start finding out about courses and scholarships? Why?

> A scholarship is money given to a student by a university or government or some other place to help with study costs. Here are some websites where you can find some information about scholarships.
>
> > www.iefa.com
> > Here international students can search for scholarships by area of study, by the country of origin, by the region where they want to study, or by the name of the university.
> >
> > www.isoa.org
> > This site is specifically for international students already living in the United States.
> >
> > www.globalgrant.com
> > Although this site charges a fee to help you find a scholarship, this kind of service may be useful when you don't have access to a university or if your university does not have someone to help you with your scholarship.

2 **Complete this sentence in your own words.**

When I think of Australia, I ---

3 **Read the first section of the homepage of OZ International Student on a website you found whilst surfing the net. Compare your sentence in Exercise 2 with the first sentence on the homepage.**

File Edit View Favorites Tools Help
Address http://www.australia.internationalstudent.com ☐ ▾ ☐ Go   Links »

OZ.International **STUDENT** .COM

International Student Exchange and Study in Australia Centre

Study Australia | Why Study Oz?

Why Study Oz?

When most people think of Australia, they see wide open spaces of outback bush, kangaroos, koalas and clean air and water. Not a bad image to be portraying to the world! However, Australia has so much more to offer than just these stereotypical offerings. What has Australia to offer to an international student?

4 **The first section on the homepage ends with a question. Before you read on, think about the answer to the question. What do you think the homepage will say?**

----

5 **Look at the section headings of the homepage below. Did you consider these topics in Exercise 4? What do you think the homepage might say about these specific topics?**

Growing Destination	Cost of Living	Technology
Global Recognition	Diversity	Work

6 **Here are the first words of the six sections. (They are in order.) How do you think the sentences might continue?**

a Australia is rapidly growing as
----

b Degrees obtained from Australian universities are ----------------------

c The cost of living and tuition fees in Australia are ----------------------
----

d Institutions in Australia offer --------
----

e Not many people know this, but
----

f The Australian immigration system allows ----------------------------
----

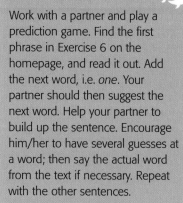

Class bonus

Work with a partner and play a prediction game. Find the first phrase in Exercise 6 on the homepage, and read it out. Add the next word, i.e. *one*. Your partner should then suggest the next word. Help your partner to build up the sentence. Encourage him/her to have several guesses at a word; then say the actual word from the text if necessary. Repeat with the other sentences.

7 **Read the rest of the homepage on the opposite page. Compare your sentences in Exercise 6 with the sentences in the homepage.**

8 **Does Australia sound like an attractive place in which to study? Would you like to live there? Why? / Why not?**

Growing Destination

Australia is rapidly growing as one of the most popular destinations for international students to attend. Currently it has the third largest international student enrolment behind the likes of the USA and the UK.

Global Recognition

Degrees obtained from Australian universities are recognized all over the world, and there is the added boost that the Australian higher education system is federally regulated. Which means the Australian government regulates all universities in the country each year to make sure they are maintaining their high education standards.

Cost of Living

The cost of living and tuition fees in Australia are much lower than compared to the USA or the UK. These lower costs make it more affordable for students to attend a school in Australia and still have a high standard of living.

Diversity

Institutions in Australia offer a wide variety of course and degrees, making it easy to find a fit that is right for you!

Technology

Not many people know this, but Australia is in the top ten spenders in the world for Research and Development and 2% of all scientific papers in the world come from Australia. This puts Australia at the forefront of new technology and innovations. From only a meagre population of 19 million, there have been 7 Nobel Prize winners.

Work

The Australian immigration system allows students visiting the country on a student visa the chance to work up to 20 hours per week during term time, and during vacations students can work full time. This opportunity makes it much more affordable for students who can attend school and still fund their education with some work.

For such a relatively young country, Australia has so much to offer an international student.

To learn more about Study in Australia, please visit:

- Why Study Oz?
- Right Program?
- Living in Oz
- Finances / Scholarships
- Post Graduation

Focus on ... abCdef
this and *these*

1 <u>Underline</u> these words in the text. What do the words refer to?

a *these stereotypical offerings* (first section)

----

b *These lower costs* (under 'Cost of Living')

----

c *This opportunity* (under 'Work')

----

2 <u>Underline</u> the words *this* and *This* in the section 'Technology'. What do they refer to?

a *this* _____

b *This* _____

In most cases, you will need to read what comes before the word(s); in one case, you will need to read on.

E✗tra practice

Look at the website www.australia.internationalstudent.com and find out what advice it gives about getting a scholarship to study in Australia.

Can-do checklist

Tick what you can do.

	Can do	Need more practice
I can interpret signalling words and phrases, and use them to understand a text.	✔	✔
I can evaluate reasons for choosing a university overseas.		
I can understand a homepage about universities in Australia.		

Unit 13
Read faster!

Get ready to read

○ Which of these statements do you agree with? Tick ✓ the boxes.
A good reader always reads at the same speed. ☐
You should focus on one word at a time. ☐
You can only understand a text if you read it slowly. ☐
You need to understand every word of what you're reading. ☐
You should always read from the first word in a text to the last. ☐
You should use a dictionary as soon as you come across an unknown word. ☐

go to Useful language p. 86

A Obstacles to faster effective reading

1 You are going to read some sections of a textbook called *Practical Faster Reading*. This book has been written for non-native speakers who are studying in English. Read the paragraph below and decide which of the following choices sums up the ideas of the paragraph. Tick ✓ one of the boxes.

a How to increase your reading speed ☐
b The advantages of a generally higher reading speed ☐
c What prevents you from achieving a higher reading speed ☐

2 Skim the passage on the opposite page. Which of the topics in Exercise 1 does it mention?

Faster effective reading

A higher reading rate, with no loss of comprehension, will help you in other subjects as well as English, and the general principles apply to any language. Naturally, you will not read every book at the same speed. You would expect to read a newspaper, for example, much more rapidly than a textbook – but you can raise your average reading speed over the whole range of materials you wish to cover so that the percentage gain will be the same whatever kind of reading you are concerned with.

Did you know ...?

People don't have just one reading rate. Although research has shown that the average high-school student in the United States reads at an average of 250 words per minute, really good readers know that reading rates need to be flexible. They learn to vary their speed from 150 to 800 words per minute, choosing their appropriate speed after considering: the difficulty of the text; their purpose in reading; their familiarity with the subject matter.

Learning tip

When you are reading, try not to let your eyes regress – do not stop and re-read words you have just read. Keep on going forwards rather than going back. If you are unsure of something, the meaning may become clear from the rest of the sentence/paragraph/text. If the meaning is still unclear when you have finished reading, you can always return to this part of the text if you think that it is vital to comprehension.

Obstacles to faster effective reading

Perhaps you have seen very young children – or older people – learning to read. They move the index finger along the line of print, pointing to each word, sometimes even to individual letters, saying the word or letters to themselves in a low voice. This is called 'vocalizing'. Sometimes the learner makes no sound though his lips may move to form the words, sometimes there is not even any perceptible movement of the mouth at all, but the
5   learner is still activating his throat muscles slightly to 'say' the words to himself. He is still vocalizing.

However slight the extent of vocalizing may be it will still be impossible for such a reader to reach a speed of more than 280 w.p.m. The appreciation of written words must be entirely visual and we must read more than one word at a time.

Look at 'you', the second word of this passage. Even if you look straight at the 'o' of that word, without
10   moving your eyes at all you can clearly see 'perhaps' and 'have' on either side. So you can read three words at once. Now look at the word 'word' on line 2. With a very slight movement of the eyes, you can take in the whole phrase '… saying the word or letters …' in the same glance. In the same way, you can probably take in a complete short sentence on one line, like the one on line 3, at one glance. None of the lines of print on a page this size should need more than four or five eye movements. Take line 4. This would perhaps break up into four
15   word groups: (1) … may move to form the words … (2) … sometimes there is not even … (3) … any perceptible movement … (4) … of the mouth at all, but the … When you are reading well, your eyes will be one or two word groups ahead of the one your mind is taking in.

Practise on something easy and interesting

Many students trying to increase their effective reading speed become discouraged when they find that if they try to race through a passage faster, they fail to take in what they have read. The problem here is that the material
20   they are practising on is either too difficult for them in vocabulary or content, or not sufficiently interesting. Read things you like reading. Go to the subject catalogue in the library. Biography, sport, the cinema … there is bound to be some area that interests you and in which you can find books of about your level of ability or just below.

If you want a quick check on how easy a book is, read through three or four pages at random. If there are, on average, more than five or six words on each page that are completely new to you, then the book is not suitable
25   for reading-speed improvement.

---

3 Read the passage from beginning to end. Do not stop and do not go back over what you have read. Then decide whether the following statements are true (T) or false (F) according to the information given in the passage.

  a Very old people and very young children learn to read in much the same way. ......

  b Vocalizing will prevent readers from reading at speeds of over 100 w.p.m. ......

  c It is sometimes possible to see three words at once without moving the eyes. ......

  d To read well, your eyes should be one or two word groups ahead of your mind. ......

  e Some students get discouraged when they first start reading faster. ......

  f It is more important to read fast than to understand what is read. ......

  g Reading practice material should be interesting and not too hard. ......

  h It is impossible to check quickly how difficult a book is. ......

  i You should never read a book that has five or six new words per page. ......

4 Check your own answers to Exercise 3 by scanning for the specific information in the passage which is related to the true/false sentences. Underline the information.

5 Look at the statements in *Get ready to read* again. Information is given for three of them in the passages on these pages. Which three? Decide whether the statements are true or false according to what you have read.

E✗tra practice

Choose a book which you would like to read, and which you can use to practise your speed reading. Bear in mind the points made in the last section of the passage when you choose your book. Keep reading!

B Hints for reading practice

1 What do you already know about how to increase your reading speed? Complete these sentences.

a .... regress.
b .... vocalize.
c .... groups.
d .... difficult.

2 Skim the passage below. How many hints are there for reading practice? What are they?

3 Read the first two sections/hints from beginning to end. Do not stop and do not go back over what you have read. Then select the answer which is most accurate according to the information given in the passage.

1 Reading words one at a time is bad because
   a all words are equally important. ☐
   b it is more difficult to get a general idea of a passage. ☐
   c some words are longer then others. ☐

2 It is a good idea to skim through a passage first
   a to get a general idea of each paragraph. ☐
   b so that you can take in each word separately. ☐
   c to make sure you get to the end at least once. ☐

3 Titles and paragraph headings
   a are more important than anything else. ☐
   b can easily be remembered without looking back. ☐
   c can help us to get the outline of a passage. ☐

4 The topic sentence of an information-giving paragraph in English
   a usually comes in the middle. ☐
   b is most likely to be found at the end. ☐
   c is most often at the beginning. ☐

5 Sometimes we know the first sentence is not the topic sentence because
   a it does not seem to give us enough new information. ☐
   b it is not long enough. ☐
   c it does not make complete sense. ☐

6 The closing paragraph of a piece of writing
   a is not really very important. ☐
   b is often unnecessary repetition. ☐
   c often summarizes the essence of the passage. ☐

4 Read the third section/hint. Complete these sentences about the third hint.

a For speed reading practice, a dictionary

....

b If you really want to know what all the words mean,

....

c Even if you don't know a word, you can often get the meaning by ....

5 Read the first section/hint again. Which of the following choices sums up the ideas of the paragraph? Tick ✓ the box.

a Advice on how to get the general idea of a piece of reading quickly. ☐
b The use of the title. ☐
c The disadvantage of an initial reading that is very careful. ☐

6 Write a summary of the second and third sections. Write phrases like those in Exercise 5.

....
....

7 Look at the statements in *Get ready to read* again. Information is given for three of them in the passage on the opposite page. Decide whether the statements are true or false according to what you have read.

Focus on ...
words in context

Try to work out from the context which words in the box replace the italicized words in the sentences.

1 peaked cap	2 foretell	3 stewpot
4 practising	5 deputies	6 amusing
7 illogical	8 seaweed	9 cave-dwellers
10 fifteenth century		

a Muhammad Ali was not fighting seriously in the gymnasium – he was only *sparring* with a friend.
b The Prince left most of the ordinary everyday decisions to his *satraps*.
c The crowd obviously enjoyed the fat man's *risible* efforts to compete in the 100 metres dash.
d The soldiers did not have plates, so they ate straight from the *dixie*.
e The fortune-teller was unable to *prognosticate* the events of the following week.
f General de Gaulle always wore a *képi* with his uniform instead of a steel helmet.
g Many early types of human being were *troglodytes* before they learned to build houses.
h Italian artists were more active in the *quattrocento* than in the sixteenth century which followed.
i The politician was embarrassed when his argument was proved to be *specious*.
j The Japanese are investigating the possibility of using marine resources such as plankton and *kelp* for human food.

Hints for reading practice

Think of the passage as a whole

When you practise reading with passages shorter than book length, like the passages in this course, do not try to take in each word separately, one after the other. It is much more difficult to grasp the broad theme of the passage this way, and you will also get stuck on individual words which may not be absolutely essential to a general understanding of the passage. It is a good idea to skim through the passage very quickly first to get the general idea of each paragraph. Titles, paragraph headings and emphasized words (underlined or in italics) can be a great help in getting this skeleton outline of the passage.

Pay attention to paragraph structure

Most paragraphs have a 'topic sentence' which expresses the central idea. The remaining sentences expand or support that idea. It has been estimated that between 60 and 90% of all information-giving paragraphs in English have the topic sentence first. Always pay special attention to the first sentence of a paragraph; it is most likely to give you the main idea.

Sometimes, though, the first sentence in the paragraph does not have the feel of a 'main idea' sentence. It does not seem to give us enough new information to justify a paragraph. The next most likely place to look for the topic sentence is the last sentence of the paragraph. Take this paragraph for example:

'Some students prefer a strict teacher who tells them exactly what to do. Others prefer to be left to work on their own. Still others like a democratic discussion type of class. No one teaching method can be devised to satisfy all students at the same time.'

Remember that the opening and closing paragraphs of a passage or chapter are particularly important. The opening paragvraph suggests the general direction and content of the piece, while the closing paragraph often summarizes the very essence of what has been said.

Dictionaries slow you down!

If you have chosen the right, fairly easy, sort of book for your general reading practice, you will not need to use a dictionary. If you really must know the dictionary meaning of all the words you meet (a doubtful necessity) jot them down on a piece of paper to look up later. Actually, the meanings of many words will be clear from the sentences around them – what we call the 'context'. Here is an example. Do you know the word 'sou'wester'? It has two meanings in English as the following sentences indicate:
a) In spite of the fact that the fishermen were wearing sou'westers, the storm was so heavy they were wet through.
b) An east or north-east wind brings cold, dry weather to England, but a sou'wester usually brings rain.
You should have guessed very easily that in sentence a) the word sou'wester refers to some kind of waterproof clothing, presumably quite thick and heavy since it is worn by fishermen in storms. In sentence b) it is clearly a kind of wind, coming from a south-westerly direction.

Class bonus
Discuss the hints in this unit with the class. Which, if any, do you need to work at more?

Can-do checklist

Tick what you can do.

	Can do	Need more practice
I can appreciate the benefits of reading faster.	✓	✓
I can overcome obstacles to faster reading.		
I can practise reading faster.		

Unit 14
I've chosen this topic

Get ready to read

- In this unit, you are going to read some extracts from a reference book. Which of the following are reference books? Tick ✓ the boxes. Can you add any others to the list?
  - a handbook ☐
  - c atlas ☐
  - b thesaurus ☐
  - d manual ☐

- You are going to read extracts from a reference book which has the following features. Put them in the order in which they should appear in the book.
  - a Chapters ☐
  - d Index ☐
  - b Introduction ☐
  - e Contents ☐
  - c Back cover ☐
  - f Front cover ☐

- Do you ever refer to reference books like the one above?

go to Useful language p. 86

A Look it up in the Index

1 **Your class is doing a project on the United States. Your teacher has asked you to research a topic and give a short talk to the class. You have been told that Americans work very long hours, so you think you might try and find out more about this topic. Here are some questions you would like to find answers to. Add another question to this list.**

   a Is it true that Americans work long hours?
   b How many hours a week do people work by law?
   c Do many people do overtime?
   d How many weeks a year does the average American work?

2 **You decide that you will probably find more reliable information about your topic in the library than on the Internet. Which of these books do you think would be most useful? Why?**

   a *Independent Traveller's USA*
   b *A Pocket History of the United States*
   c *The Kennedy Women*
   d *Contemporary America*

3 **You pick up *Contemporary America*. Skim the back cover of the book on the right and decide if this book might be worth looking at.**

Review of the first edition

'Clear and well-balanced ... All the basics anyone seeking an overview of the nation's major contours are here ... Anyone reading the volume – whether new student or experienced scholar – will come away from it better informed.' **Dale Carter**, *The Newsletter of the Nordic Association for American Studies*

This completely revised and updated second edition of Contemporary America provides an extremely broad-ranging introduction to the society, politics, economy, culture, and world role of the United States.

Russell Duncan is Professor of American History and Social Sciences, The English Institute, University of Copenhagen. He has written nine books and many articles on various aspects of American culture and history.

Joseph Goddard is a graduate student at The English Institute, University of Copenhagen, where he has taught courses on the American City and American Politics and Society.

ISBN 0-403-94864-9

9 780403 948642

Learning tip

In the classroom, we are usually given the texts we need to read. Sometimes, however, we need to actually find the best extract within a book for our purposes. Use a mixture of skimming and scanning to find out if a book is suitable and likely to provide you with the information you are looking for; skim the back cover to get an overall feel for the book; scan the Contents and the Index to find your topic; then go to the pages that are mentioned in the Index to find the entry (word from the Index) you are looking for; and skim the text around the word. Then decide how useful the text is for your task.

4 The book *Contemporary America* has ten chapters. The back cover mentions five of the main topics. Find and <u>underline</u> them.

5 Look at the Contents page on the right. Are the five topics mentioned?

6 Look at the Contents page again. Answer these questions.

 a Which of the chapters do you think would be most useful for the topic mentioned in Exercise 1?

 b Do any of the chapter headings – or sub-headings – use the word *work*?

7 Look in the Index below for the word *work*. Answer these questions.

 a Is the word *work* in the Index as an entry?

 b Which of the entries do you think might be the most useful to you in researching the topic in Exercise 1?

8 Look at the page numbers for the entry *working hours* and find out which of the nine main chapters deals with the topic. Is this the same chapter you identified in Exercise 6?

Contents

B This looks useful

1 According to the Index, the topic of working hours is on pages 220–1 and 272. There are no references to working hours in the first paragraph on page 220. Extract A is the second paragraph. How many references to working hours are there? <u>Underline</u> the information in the paragraph.

2 Does the information in Extract A answer any of your questions in Exercise 1 on page 64? Which one(s)?

3 Extract B is the next paragraph (this one is on page 221). <u>Underline</u> the information about working hours.

Did you know ...?

Double speech marks, as in "overwhelmed", are more common in US English than in UK English.

4 Do you think most Americans work 40 hours a week or do they work more? Do not check your answers at this stage.

5 Extract C is the first sentence of the next paragraph on page 221. Do you think this paragraph is going to be about working hours?

6 The topic of working hours is also mentioned on page 272. Look at the Contents page on page 65 of this unit. Which chapter is this in?

A   Laws prevent employers from discriminating in hiring on the basis of age, sex, race, religion, physical handicaps, or national origin. There are laws to maintain safe working conditions and to allow release time for childbirth, adoption, or to care for sick relatives. The United States has had a federally-mandated work week and minimum wage since 1938, when the maximum hours an individual can be required to work was set at 40 hours and the base wages put at $0.25 an hour. In 2005, all full-time workers over 18 years old were guaranteed at least $5.15 an hour; those under 18, or those in jobs where tips made up a large part of their salaries might receive less. At minimum wage, a full-time (40-hours-a-week) worker would make $206 a week before taxes. Moreover, 12 states have laws putting minimum wages above the national requirement. Washington sets it at $7.16, Connecticut at $7.10, and California at $6.75, for example (DOL, 2005). Most businesses pay higher wages than are required by law, usually about $7 an hour for beginners. In 2000, the average hourly pay for all US wage and salaried workers was $16.17 an hour (AP, 2001d). Any work done beyond the 40-hour maximum is subject to overtime pay at a higher rate of 1.5 to 2 times the hourly rate. In 2004, the average worker took home three hours of overtime pay per week.

B   One in three American workers say that they are "overwhelmed" with the amount of work required of them (Joyner, 2001). With technological advances speeding up assembly lines, companies have "downsized" the number of workers while asking them to increase output by working faster and longer. Part of the problem has been that with personal consumption – with high home mortgages and transportation costs – and the fears of an economic slowdown male workers work harder to prove their worth. Those who work long hours hope to be among those retained if and when downsizing comes. Of course, this is a numbers game as two in three workers do not feel overwhelmed, say that they are satisfied with their jobs, and do not fear layoffs (Harris Poll, 2000d). Beyond the office, technology is affecting hours as e-mail, voice recorders, and cellphones allow the job to spill over into home life. Additionally, the average two-way commute nationwide adds 48 minutes to the workday. For those working in big cities like New York and living in the suburbs, commutes can often total 1.5 hours each way.

C   About 15 percent of the labor force is in motion in any given year, selling their skills in the marketplace to the highest bidder as they change employers and geographical locations.

7 **Extract D is a sentence about working hours from page 272. Are the figures bigger or smaller than you expected?**

8 **You decide to look up the word *holidays* in the Index, as this might help you to find out how much time Americans spend not working. Extract E is what you find on page 196. Does this information surprise you at all?**

9 **Is it true that Americans work very long hours? How do their working hours compare with those in your own country?**

D   Americans work about 350 hours more per year (9 weeks) than their European counterparts.

E   American workers generally take between one week (business and manufacturing firms) and four weeks (teachers and government workers) of paid vacation a year. Nationwide, companies have downsized free time to an average of only 8.1 days off after a one-year employment period, and 10.2 days after three years on the job. Additionally, 13 percent of US companies allow leave, but without pay (Robinson, 2003). There are also growing numbers of people trapped in the work-and-spend cycle or who have not just a work ethic – but an overwork ethic – and so opt for nothing longer than a weekend getaway now and then.

E ✗ tra practice

Research a topic connected with the United States or another English-speaking country of your choice. Select a topic that interests you. Find a book in the library or look for information on the Internet.

Class bonus

Take turns to give a short talk about the topic you have researched.

Focus on ...
US English

1 What are the UK English equivalents of the words *labor force* and *vacation*?

2 Read these sentences from *Contemporary America*. Circle the US English words.
   a It might be easier to think of the middle class as being composed of those people who have at least a *high-school / secondary school* education.
   b There is a nostalgia for the mythical good old days when women stayed *at home / home*, men went to work, children were manageable and "above average" and two cars were in every driveway.
   c Most teens get driver's *licences / licenses* when they are 16 and, quickly thereafter, a car of their own.
   d Most American families in the 1990s neither had a family budget nor saved money for the future; instead, they spent their entire salaries between *paychecks / pay cheques* and bought on credit.
   e The poor are concentrated into inner-city *neighbourhoods / neighborhoods*.

3 The sentences above are all from one chapter in *Contemporary America*. Look at the Contents list on page 65 and work out which chapter.

Can-do checklist

Tick what you can do.

	Can do	Need more practice
I can skim the back cover in order to assess the suitability of a book for my studies.		
I can scan the Contents and Index, and find the entries within the book.		
I can assess the suitability of text extracts for my purposes.		
I can make notes on the main points of text extracts.		

Unit 15
English today

Get ready to read

○ Read these sentences about the English language. Complete the sentences with the numbers in the box. (You will have to write some of them as words.)

| 1 | 3 | 4 | 40 | 70 | 600 | 1,700 | 800,000 |

a   Of all the languages in the world, English has the largest vocabulary – about .... words.
b   .... per cent of webpages are written in English.
c   .... is the only number which has its letters in alphabetical order.
d   .... is the only number with its letters in reverse alphabetical order.
e   The first known use of about .... words or meanings is in the works of William Shakespeare.
f   .... is the only number whose number of letters in the word equals the number.
g   Only .... words in the English language end with the letters 'ceed'.
h   French was the official language of England for over .... years.

go to Useful language p. 86

A English as a foreign language

1 In this unit you are going to read some extracts from a book called *The English Language*. Chapter 1 is about the number of people in the world who speak English. Paragraph 1 is from the first part of this chapter. Read paragraph 1. Do we know how many people speak English as a foreign or as a second language?

2 What do you understand by 'the tip of a very large iceberg'?

3 Paragraph 2 is from the third part of chapter 1. Read paragraph 2. Are you part of this group of English speakers?

4 Who does the first part of the language-learning iceberg relate to? <u>Underline</u> words in the extract which give the answer.

> 1   Finding out about the number of foreigners using English isn't easy, and that is why there is so much variation among the estimates. There are hardly any official figures. No one knows how many foreign people have learned English to a reasonable standard of fluency – or to any standard at all, for that matter. There are a few statistics available – from examination boards, for example – but these are only the tip of a very large iceberg.

> 2   The second part of the language-learning iceberg relates to people who live in countries where English has no official status, but where it is learned as a foreign language in schools and institutes of higher education, and through the use of a wide range of 'self-help' materials. There are only hints as to what the numbers involved might be. Even in the statistically aware countries of Western Europe, there are no reliable figures available for the number of people who are learning English as a foreign language – or any other language, for that matter. In a continent such as South America, the total is pure guesswork.

Learning tip

In general, a paragraph deals with a single topic – for example, an event, a description, or an idea. It usually – but not always – contains a topic sentence (one that sums up the main point of the paragraph). If you can identify the topic, the main point, and the minor or supporting points, then you have understood the organization of the paragraph. If you can identify how the author links one paragraph to the next, then you will see how the author's ideas hang together. This will make the text more accessible to you.

5 There is no topic sentence in paragraph 2. Which of these sentences is the main point of the paragraph? Tick ✓ the correct box.

a It is impossible to know how many people are learning English because there are no reliable figures available. ☐

b Figures mentioned can only be estimates as the number of people learning English is increasing all the time. ☐

c We can only find out how many people are learning English in indirect ways. ☐

6 Skim the extract below. These paragraphs follow paragraph 2. Which group(s) of people is this extract about? Tick ✓ the correct box.

a speakers of English as a foreign language ☐

b speakers of English as a second language ☐

c both of the above groups ☐

3 Totals cited in the 1990s ranged from 300–400 million to over a billion, the latter (in a British Council estimate) based largely on the figures available from English-language examining boards, estimates of listeners to English-language radio programmes, sales of English-language newspapers, and the like. The figures are vague because it is notoriously difficult to decide the point at which an English learner has learned 'enough' English to be counted as a reasonably fluent speaker. Also, the published statistics are unable to keep up with the extraordinary growth in learning English in many countries. In particular, it is difficult to obtain a precise notion about what is currently happening in China.

4 In China, there has been an explosion of interest in the English language in recent years. In 1983, it is thought, around 100 million people watched the television series designed to teach the language, *Follow Me*. Considerable publicity was given in the Western media to the sight of groups of Chinese practising English-language exercises after work, or queuing to try out their English on a passing tourist. The presenter of *Follow Me*, Kathy Flower, became a national celebrity, recognized everywhere. And the interest continues, with a new series of programmes being designed to meet the needs of scientific and business users. What level of fluency is being achieved by this massive influx of learners is unknown. But if only a fraction of China's population is successful, this alone will be enough to make a significant impact on the total for world foreign-language use.

5 And why shouldn't they be successful, in China, Japan, Brazil, Poland, Egypt, and elsewhere? There is enormous motivation, given the way that English has become the dominant language of world communication. Textbooks on English these days regularly rehearse the litany of its achievements. It is the main language of the world's books, newspapers, and advertising. It is the official international language of airports and air traffic control. It is the chief maritime language. It is the language of international business and academic conferences, of diplomacy, of sport. Over two thirds of the world's scientists write in English. Three quarters of the world's mail is written in English. Eighty per cent of all information stored in the electronic retrieval systems of the world is stored in English. And, at a local level, examples of the same theme can be found everywhere. A well-known Japanese company, wishing to negotiate with its Arabic customers, arranges all its meetings in English. A Colombian doctor reports that he spends almost as much of his time improving his English as practising medicine. A Copenhagen university student comments: 'Nearly everyone in Denmark speaks English; if we didn't, there wouldn't be anyone to talk to.'

7 Start with paragraph 2. Read the last sentence of each of paragraphs 2–4. Which word – or closely related word – is then repeated in the first sentence of the next paragraph? Circle the word.

8 There is no topic sentence in paragraph 3. Which of the sentences in Exercise 5 is the main point of the paragraph?

9 Identify and underline the topic sentence in paragraphs 4 and 5. This sentence should make the main point of the paragraph.

10 Circle the examples in paragraphs 3–5 which support the main point.

paragraph 3   1 example
paragraph 4   2 examples
paragraph 5   7 general examples, 3 specific examples

11 Can you add any more examples of your own to the final paragraph?

Class bonus

Think about the reasons why you are learning English. Discuss your reasons with a partner. Then make a list of reasons for the whole class.

B English loan words

1 Read the first sentence of the extract *English loan words*. Which words do you think were in the final sentence of the preceding paragraph? Tick ✓ one of the boxes.

a best-known example ☐
b language change ☐
c English words ☐

Did you know …?

About 240 million Americans (85% of the US population) speak English as their mother tongue. In addition, there are approximately 115 million native speakers in Britain, Ireland, Australia, New Zealand, Canada and South Africa.

Focus on …
participle adjectives

1 Complete this sentence from the text on the right.
The American way of life is considered modern, fashionable, and desirable to the younger, trend-setting generations of society found in all .... and .... countries.
Note that the missing words are both participles – the first means 'countries which are developing' and the second means 'countries which have (been) developed'.

2 Circle the correct participle in these sentences.
a The police recovered the *stealing / stolen* goods.
b Don't wake the *sleeping / slept* child.
c I got very *disappointing / disappointed* exam results.
d That is really *surprising / surprised* news!
e The *proposing / proposed* road scheme is not very popular.
f Our *renting / rented* TV blew up two days after we got it.

English loan words

1 The best-known example of external influence causing language change is the 'Americanization' of world culture, which has caused English words to appear prominently in city streets all over the world, reflecting the dominance of that culture's popular songs, films, television, high finance, food and drink, and consumer goods. The American way of life is considered modern, fashionable, and desirable to the younger, trend-setting generations of society found in all developed and developing countries, and the language associated with these trends is eagerly taken up. The effect is most noticeable in pop music. Foreign groups often record in English, and the words are picked up and rehearsed in the same language everywhere, even by children who otherwise have little or no command of the language. I once met a Brazilian child of about ten who could count 'one, two, three', but only by adding the words 'o'clock, four o'clock rock' at the end.

2 Answer these questions about the paragraph above.

a What is the topic?
b Which is the topic sentence (or main point)?
c How many examples does the paragraph give to support its main point?

3 Read the text below and answer these questions.

a Are any of these loan words used in your language?
b Can you add any more words for each category?
c Can you think of any words for the categories *sport* and *tourism/transport*?

English loan words in Europe

All the words below have been found in various European languages without any translation being given. The spelling below is standard English; different countries re-spell a word according to its own conventions, e.g. *boxing* becomes *boksing* in Norwegian, *goal* becomes *gowl* in Spanish. Also several languages adapt English words to their own grammar, e.g. Italian *weekendista*, *cocacolonizzare* (Coca-Cola colonize).

Politics, commerce: big business, boom, briefing, dollar, good-will, marketing, new deal, senator, sterling, top secret

Culture, entertainment: cowboy, group, happy ending, heavy metal, hi-fi, jam session, jazz, juke-box, Miss World (etc.), musical, night-club, ping-pong, pop, rock, showbiz, soul, top twenty, Western, yeah-yeah-yeah

People and behaviour: AIDS, angry young man, baby-sitter, boy friend, boy scout, cool, crazy, dancing, gangster, hold-up, jogging, reporter, smart, snob, teenager

Consumer society: air conditioner, all rights reserved, aspirin, bar, bestseller, bulldozer, camera, chewing gum, Coca Cola, cocktail, drive-in, eye-liner, film, hamburger, hoover, jumper, ketchup, kingsize, Kleenex, layout, Levis, make-up, sandwich, science fiction, Scrabble, self-service, smoking, snackbar, supermarket, tape, thriller, up-to-date, WC, weekend.

And of course: OK

4 Paragraphs 2–4 on the right follow paragraph 1. Read paragraphs 2–4. Identify the topic and topic sentence (or main point) of each paragraph and give examples.

5 Can you add any more examples of your own to the three paragraphs?

6 What is your reaction to any of the points made in this text?

7 Imagine you have to write an essay: *How important is the English language in your life?* Which, if any, of the points made in the extracts in this unit would you include in your essay?

E Xtra practice

When you are reading a text in English, note down any words that are used in your own language. Are the words used with the same meaning – or are they 'false friends'? For example, the words *jeans, pullover, bowling, goal* and *picnic* are all used in Greek with the same meaning. However, words like *agenda* (the Greek meaning is 'notebook'), *air* (meaning 'wind') and *sympathise* (meaning 'like') are all false friends – their meaning is not the same in both languages. Try and avoid using false friends.

2   Depending on your point of view, therefore, English loan words are a good thing or a bad thing. People who do not approve of American values or who are disturbed by rapidity of change are often strongly critical of the impact of English on their language – especially when an English word supplants a traditional word. For example, in Spanish, *planta* ('plant', in the sense of 'factory') is often used where *fabrica* (factory) was used before, and this has been criticized in the press and on television. Similarly, in Dutch, *mistletoe* is now often found where *maretak* was used before. In 1977, France passed a law banning the use of English words in official contexts if an equivalent French expression existed – but the law seems to be honoured more in the breach than in the observance. Some other countries have considered introducing a similar law – for example, Brazil in 2000, Germany in 2001 – despite the evidence that such laws have very little effect, and that the arrival of loan words can greatly enrich a language (as indeed in the case of English itself, which has a long history of welcome for foreign words; see p. 40).

3   However, not everyone is critical. In particular, commercial firms and advertisers are well aware of the potential selling power that the use of English vocabulary can bring. There have been several reports of an increase in sales once a firm has given a product an English name (in much the same way as some products are given foreign names in Britain – such as French names for scent). In Japan, English is even used in television commercials, despite the fact that the majority of viewers would not understand exactly what was being said: the prestige connotations attached to the mere use of English are apparently enough to command the strategy to the advertisers. Nor is it purely a matter of commerce. In one Dutch town, the leader of a youth club gave his club an English name, and there was an immediate increase in the active interest of the boys in the area.

4   Most of the influence of English is upon the vocabulary of foreign languages; but surveys are slowly bringing to light several cases where word order or word structure has been affected. Sentences of the type 'The book sells well', using an active construction for a passive meaning, have begun to appear in Danish (*Bogen soelger godt*). Several languages keep the English plural ending when they make use of a loan word, and do not translate it into the native form, e.g. drinks, cocktails. An indefinite article is sometimes used in Swedish sentences like *Han är en lakare* (He is a doctor), where previously it would not have appeared. English word endings sometimes compete with foreign ones (e.g. *eskalation* alongside *eskalering* in Danish). There are many other such cases.

Can-do checklist

Tick what you can do.

	Can do	Need more practice
I can identify how a paragraph is organized.	✓	
I can use my knowledge of paragraph organization to help me understand a text.	✓	
I can distinguish between the main points of a paragraph/text and examples.		✓

Unit 16
I need a good score

Get ready to read

● Imagine you are about to take an English language exam. Which of these papers would you be most worried about? Put them in order. (1 = most worried, 2 = least worried)
Listening ☐
Reading ☐
Writing ☐
Speaking ☐

● Many people who want to study at an English-language university take the IELTS exam. Your teacher tells you about four of the exam tasks you might have to do in two of the IELTS tests. Which paper(s) is he/she talking about?
a   true / false / not given
b   sentence completion
c   labelling a diagram
d   multiple choice

go to Useful language p. 86

A Exam practice tasks

Did you know ...?

You cannot pass or fail the IELTS exam. The university or college that you wish to enter will inform you of the overall IELTS Band Score they require for enrolment in the particular course you wish to study. You will be given a mark between 0 and 9 for each of the four Sub-tests (Listening, Reading, Writing, Speaking). Your overall Band Score is an average of the four Sub-test Band Scores. As a guideline, Business students generally need a score of around 6.5. If you want to improve your score, you can take the exam as many times as you like. However, you must wait a minimum of three months before taking the test again.

Learning tip

The IELTS Reading Sub-test is in three sections. There are three passages with a combined length of 2000–2750 words and a total of 40 questions. You have only one hour to answer the questions – there is quite a risk that you will run out of time. Your aim is not to understand the writer's message but to answer the questions. This is your purpose in reading and it should determine the way you read the text. Always have a question in mind when you read the text – and give yourself a reason for reading.

1 In this unit you are going to practise summary completion. Candidates may have to complete a summary in an IELTS Reading test. Skim this section of the unit and find out how many types of summary-completion task there are.

2 Here is an extract from a book called *Action Plan For IELTS*. Study the 'Summary completion' box and the 'Action plan' before and while you do the task on the opposite page.

> **SUMMARY COMPLETION**
> You complete the summary by writing no more than three words and/ or a number from the passage in each gap. The summary may cover the ideas in the whole passage or may be based on a section of the passage only. You may be told which part it relates to. The answers may not be in passage order.

ACTION PLAN

▶ Read the instructions carefully to see how many words you can write, and whether you are told which paragraph(s) the summary comes from.
▶ Read the summary heading (if there is one) to help you find the right place in the passage.
▶ Read through the summary to get an idea of what it is about and how much of the passage it covers.
▶ Decide what kind of word is needed to complete the first gap, e.g. a noun, a name, an adjective.
▶ Note any grammatical clues, e.g. articles or prepositions, which may help you find the answer.
▶ Underline or highlight the key words around the gap.
▶ Read the passage quickly and decide where the answer to the first question comes from.
▶ Decide exactly which words or numbers you should write as your answer.
▶ Read above and below this part to find the rest of your answers.

NOW TRY THIS TASK

Complete the summary below.
*Choose **NO MORE THAN TWO WORDS AND/OR A NUMBER** from the reading passage for each answer.*

Sprawling systems on the edge of IT chaos

The UK government is at the forefront of a £10 million programme aimed at finding ways to stop catastrophic failures occurring in large IT networks. Some systems are now so large they are untestable, making it impossible to predict how they will behave under all circumstances. The hidden errors could lead to crashes in critical networks like healthcare or banking systems.

The scheme has been given added urgency by the failures of power grids in the US and Italy last year. 'The system failures in terms of electricity blackouts show that patterns of unexpected and negative behaviour can arise, and when they do they are often disastrous,' says the government's chief scientist, David King. If a century-old technology like a power grid can fail, the same might easily happen to modern IT methods.

Taking precautions

The government has set up a scheme at a cost of (1) .... to investigate ways of preventing large IT (2) .... Because they are very (3) .... , the systems cannot always be tested and the fear is that hidden problems could interrupt essential services such as health and (4) .... According to the government's chief scientist, the effects of these electricity blackouts could be (5) ....

Find words or phrases in the reading passage about IT networks that have been replaced by the following words in the summary.

6 scheme   _____
7 investigate ways of preventing   _____
8 cannot always be tested   _____
9 essential services   _____
10 According to   _____

3 There is an example of a similar – but slightly different – exam task below. This summary is also based on the text *Sprawling systems on the edge of IT chaos*. Read the instructions and carry out the task.

Complete the summary using the list of words A–J.

The government has established a £10 million programme designed to prevent potentially catastrophic IT failures. This is because the (11) .... of some systems makes it very difficult to (12) .... them accurately. The idea has been given (13) .... following the electrical failures in America and Europe last year, which were due to the considerable (14) .... of the grids.

A	test	F	repair
B	build	G	priority
C	measure	H	importance
D	age	I	funding
E	size	J	condition

15 Which words in the passage helped you choose the correct words from the box?

E✗tra practice

Go to the IELTS website www.ielts.org and find out more about the IELTS exam. Would you be interested in taking it?

Focus on ...
paraphrasing

In exam tasks like the one in Exercise 3, you need to recognize synonyms or groups of words that paraphrase ideas in the passage. Read these sentences and find words or phrases that have been used instead of the unused words in the list in Exercise 3. Write the letters in the boxes. Then rewrite part of each sentence.

a Even after a week in the desert, she was in great shape. ☐ J   *she was in great condition*
b We didn't realise how significant our exam results would be ☐ ....
c The man told me it would cost too much to get my bike mended. ☐ ....
d Some people get scholarships to help them with further study. ☐ ....
e Book sales are not always a way of judging their quality. ☐ ....
f They want to create a first-rate university department. ☐ ....

B Putting it into practice

1 You are going to read an IELTS exam passage and do two summary-completion tasks from a book called *Insight into IELTS*. Before you read the passage, remind yourself of the way to approach these types of task by reading the Action Plan on page 72 again.

2 Now read the passage below and carry out the tasks on the opposite page.

Soft centres – hard profits

● ● ● ● ● ● ● ● ● ● ● ● ● ● Are you being seduced by the sweet industry? ● ● ● ● ● ● ● ● ● ● ● ● ●

If chocolate were found to be seriously addictive, then the UK would need major therapy to kick the habit. The British lead the world in their love of the cocoa-based treat. As a product, chocolate has a lot going for it, appealing to all ages, both sexes and all income brackets. In 1997, the value of the total UK confectionery market increased by 3% to a staggering £5.2bn, with chocolate sales accounting for 70%, at £3.6bn, and sugar confectionery the remaining 1.6bn.

The UK market has shown consistent growth – increasing over the last decade by around 16%. 'Chocolate confectionery is a market that seems to be remarkably resilient,' says Pamela Langworthy, marketing manager for Thorntons, the luxury chocolate producer and retailer. It also increasingly transcends national boundaries. In 1997, Swiss Nestlé, the largest confectioner, exported over a quarter of its production to more than 100 countries. Nestlé has recorded particularly fast growth in confectionery sales in Asia, with expansion of KitKat into several countries in the region. Eastern Europe provides another promising market. But few markets challenge the UK in terms of current confectionery consumption. In the US, the land associated with excess, each American devours a mere 10kg of confectionery per person a year, whereas UK consumers each manage 16kg. In Europe, where the chocolate market is estimated to be worth over £12bn ($18.5bn), the UK accounts for almost a third of that total, followed some way behind by Germany, France and Italy.

Around 60% of all confectionery is bought on impulse, which makes its availability a key determinant of sales. Impulse buying also makes the development of a strong brand image vital, and large, long-established brands dominate the market. Building up these brands costs serious money. Media expenditure on confectionery exceeds that for any other impulse market. The Cadbury & Trebor Bassett 1997 *Confectionery Review* reveals that in 1996 media expenditure on chocolate reached £94m, compared with £69m spent on soft drinks, £31m on the lottery and £23m on crisps and snacks.

Innovation is also essential for ongoing success, despite the chocolate market being dominated by consistent performers. In 1996 the chocolate company Mars launched 'Flyte' claiming to be their first mainstream brand to address the demand for lower fat products. At 98 calories a bar, Flyte is designed to appeal to weight-conscious women. Another 1997 Mars launch, Celebrations, is claimed by the company's annual review to be showing signs of 'revolutionising the boxed chocolates market by attracting new, younger customers'. 'Traditonally, the boxed chocolates market hasn't changed very much. People who buy these products tend to be older and female. With Celebrations, we are finding that younger people and men are buying because the chocolates don't come in the traditional-shaped box – they look different. Products such as Flyte and Celebrations are attempts to introduce a new product category and increase sales for retailers, rather than just shifting market share,' a Mars spokesman says.

One feature of the chocolate industry in recent years has been the emergence of special editions. The concept is a marketing triumph. Producers believe that special editions offer the consumer a new and exciting variation of a product, while suggesting the same consistent quality they associate with familiar brands. Since special editions are only available for a few weeks while stocks last, they also have a unique quality about them. Far from denting sales of the straight version, limited editions appear to simply boost overall sales.

Questions 1–5

Complete the summary below.
*Choose **ONE OR TWO WORDS OR A NUMBER** from the passage for each answer.*

Chocolate – the figures

The chocolate market in the UK in 1997 was worth (1) .... , having shown a steady increase during the preceding ten-year period. Overall the manufacturer Swiss Nestlé supplies chocolate to over (2) .... and the company has seen rapid growth in the markets in (3) .... Nevertheless, the UK market remains the biggest. Surprisingly, British consumers devour more than their (4) .... counterparts and, in terms of the European chocolate market, their consumption amounts to (5) .... of the total revenue.

Questions 6–13

Complete the summary below using words from the box.

According to the passage, the chocolate market is dominated by (6) .... brands. For this reason, confectioners spend large sums of money on (7) .... advertisements. In fact, in 1996, the amount spent totalled £94m.

However, it is also important for companies to allocate resources to developing (8) .... ideas. One example of this is the 'Flyte' bar, which was developed by Mars. Chocolate producers also try to increase sales by changing their customers' (9) .... habits. For example, if a product has an (10) .... image, it may be necessary to alter this.

A (11) .... switch in consumer behaviour can be achieved by introducing 'special edition' brands on to the market. These are successful because they offer (12) .... value. They also seem to increase the (13) .... sales of standard brands.

media	new	purchasing	outstanding	impulse	children's
limited	low-fat	serious	similar	well-known	novelty	outdated
overseas	eating	international	temporary	overall	

---

3 How easy/difficult did you find the tasks? Do you feel that you are ready to take the exam – or do you need further practice?

Class bonus

Write some TRUE / FALSE / NOT GIVEN sentences about the text. Exchange your sentences with a partner. Decide if the information in your partner's sentences is true, false or not given.

E✗tra practice

Go to the library and find an IELTS book – either a self-study book, a coursebook or a book of hints. Find out what other test types there are in the Reading test. Note any useful tips.

Can-do checklist

Tick what you can do.

	Can do	Need more practice
I can follow exam tips and put them into practice.		
I can understand paraphrases.		
I can carry out exam tasks.		

A Are these statements true (T) or false (F)?

1 Some aspects of a text may not be clear to you because you do not have enough background knowledge. ...... (Unit 7)

2 If you think about the topic of a text before you read it, you can sometimes predict what it might say. ...... (Unit 8)

3 Sentences in formal texts are, in general, shorter than those in more neutral texts. ...... (Unit 9)

4 Technical texts often contain nouns used together in groups. ...... (Unit 10)

5 To get an impression of the content of a text, you can look at the headings before you begin reading. ...... (Unit 11)

6 There is no need to pay much attention to words like *however, therefore, furthermore.* ...... (Unit 12)

7 If you come across something you do not understand in a text, it is best to immediately read again what you have just read. ...... (Unit 13)

8 You need only refer to the Index when you have finished reading a book. ...... (Unit 14)

9 Paragraphs always contain one sentence that sums up the main point of the paragraph. ...... (Unit 15)

10 When you are doing an exam, you should focus on finding the information needed to answer the questions. ...... (Unit 16)

B Now read the *Learning tips* for Units 7–16 on pages 89–91. Do you want to change any of your answers in Exercise A?

C Skim texts A–D. Decide which text each person below would read. Write the letter of the text in the boxes.

11 someone who has taken on a new role at work ☐

12 someone who is interested in finding out about the company they work for ☐

13 someone who is going to take an exam ☐

14 someone who is going to study at an English-speaking university ☐

Text A

How strictly is IELTS marked?

Candidates should take care when writing answers on the Listening and Reading Answer Sheets as incorrect spelling and grammar are penalised. Both UK and US varieties of spelling are acceptable.

If candidates are asked to write an answer using a certain number of words and/or (a) number(s), they will be penalised if they exceed or do not meet this requirement. For example if a question specifies an answer using NO MORE THAN THREE WORDS and the correct answer is 'black leather coat', the answer 'coat of black leather' is incorrect.

In questions where candidates are expected to complete a gap, candidates should only transfer the necessary missing word(s) on to the Answer Sheet. For example if a candidate has to complete 'in the ....' and the correct answer is 'morning', the answer 'in the morning' would be incorrect.

Candidates should read and follow the instructions and questions very carefully. In Listening especially, care should be taken when transferring answers on to the Answer Sheet.

More samples of IELTS test material and information about the test are available on the IELTS web site: www.ielts.org

Text B

Hi all

As I'm sure you are aware, we have got out of the habit of regular fire evacuation drills. A review of the Fire Marshal procedures is well overdue. Having looked at the levels of cover, we have asked some of you to take up this role for the first time. In addition, some of the existing FMs may need a recap of where we are.

I would be grateful if you would attend a short training course on 'The Role of the Fire Marshal'. We will cover what your responsibilities are as a FM and what we expect of you in an evacuation situation. We will also cover what the plans are once we are outside etc.

The date I have in mind is Thursday 30th March (10am–11.30am). If this date is not suitable, please let me know and I will either come and see you on a one-to-one basis or run another session if a few of you cannot make it.

Kind regards
Michael Hansen
Health & Safety Manager

Text C

▶**Tutorials**

As well as lectures, many subjects have tutorials once every two or three weeks. They are smaller than lectures and students have more chance of getting to know one another.

What are tutorials for?

So far we have talked about large classes, but many courses have tutorials too. As well as being smaller than lectures, tutorials are often taught by different staff. Tutorials have several purposes, all of them to do with talking:

• to discuss the lectures;
• to exchange opinions about course readings;
• to work on group assignments;
• to discuss assignments;
• to ask questions.

Look in your departmental handbook or listen to the tutor on the first day of class to see what your subject teachers believe is important about tutorials.

The purpose of a tutorial is to talk, because talking is one way of learning. Another reason for everyone talking is to make the learning more enjoyable. If only two or three students speak, the tutorial can become boring.

Text D

Food retail

The Food Retail Group has been able to capitalise on the buoyant consumer market over the summer which was created by a combination of the excellent weather and the World Cup. By ensuring that we had the right products, at the right price, in stores over this period, we have achieved real like-for-like growth in sales and a strengthening of our profitability.

A key element of our strategy is the investment we make in our stores. This has continued during this period with a new store in Long Hanborough, near Oxford, and refits in our stores in Ladygrove, Didcot and Penkridge. All of these stores were fitted out to the new Co-operative Brand standard. For a number of years our store in Cowley has been under consideration for a full refit. It is therefore pleasing to be able to report that the directors have approved a £2 million refurbishment for this store which will be completed in time for the Christmas trading period.

If we are to compete effectively against our high street rivals, it is essential that we have an efficient food distribution system. In order to achieve this, we are going to make a significant investment into the facilities at our Distribution Depot in Oxford. This investment will improve both the cost effectiveness and the efficiency of the depot thereby strengthening our whole retail offer.

We anticipate that the second half of the year will be a challenge with all our competitors attempting to increase their market share. However, the restructuring that has taken place since the merger has, we believe, sharpened our focus and put us in a far stronger position to respond.

D Read Text A again. In which of these cases will you lose marks in the Listening and Reading tests? (Y = yes, N = no)

15 if you write *when he were given* as one of your answers ☐
16 if you use *vacation* instead of *holiday* in your writing ☐
17 if you use fewer than the specified number of words ☐
18 if you copy a word that is already given as part of the answer ☐

E Read Text B again. Are these sentences true (T) or false (F)?

19 The main purpose of the email is to remind Fire Marshals about evacuation drills. ......
20 The session is for both old and new Fire Marshals. ......
21 If one person can't go to the session, Michael Hansen will train this person on their own. ......
22 If more than one person can't go, the date of the session will be changed. ......

F Read Text C again. Answer these questions. Write a maximum of six words.

23 How often do students usually have a tutorial?
----
24 What's the best time to find out the staff's views of tutorials?
----
25 What is the main purpose of a tutorial?
----
26 Why might some students complain that they are bored in a tutorial?

G Read Text D again. Choose the best headings for the paragraphs. Write the letters in the boxes. (There are four extra headings.)

27 paragraph 1 ☐
28 paragraph 2 ☐
29 paragraph 3 ☐
30 paragraph 4 ☐

a New stores
b Increase in profits
c The futurev
d Prices and products
e The market
f Stores
g High Street rivalry
h Food distribution

H Latif works in a large supermarket. He is looking at the staff handbook. Skim the text and answer this question.

31 What is this part of the handbook about? Tick ✓ one of the boxes.
  a Having time off ☐
  b Hours of work ☐
  c Timekeeping and attendance ☐

Notification of absence

1 You should inform your immediate supervisor or manager as soon as possible on the first day of absence that you are unable to work. This notification must be made at the earliest opportunity, with the reason for the absence and the likely date of return.

2 If you cannot make contact with us yourself, you must ensure someone else notifies us on your behalf, e.g. mother, father, partner, adult son or daughter. Please note: a friend is not acceptable; neither are text messages nor emails. The person should also give some indication of how soon they expect you to return to work and the reason for your absence.

3 In the event of circumstances not permitting you to report as noted, you should ensure notification to your place of work not later than one hour from the start of your shift. If you do not follow this procedure, you may lose sick pay.

4 Upon your return, we will require self-certification for periods of absence of up to one week; medical certificates will be required for periods exceeding one week. You can obtain a self-certification form from your manager or supervisor, and he/she is entitled to ask questions about your absence. The manager will certainly want to verify the information you gave on the form by conducting a return to work interview.

Absence before or following a public holiday

5 If you are absent on the working day before or following a public holiday, you will not receive pay for the period of absence – which will include the whole of the public holiday period – unless you can prove a reasonable cause to our satisfaction. In cases of sickness, this may mean that you will have to provide a medical certificate covering the period of absence.

Long term sickness absence

6 If you are absent from work and are unable to indicate when you will return, you may be requested to attend absence review meetings with your manager in order to consider the circumstances surrounding your continued absence. Reviews may also determine whether your employment should be continued or terminated on the grounds of capability.

7 During a period of sickness absence you are expected to act responsibly in light of any medical advice given and to refrain from the following:
• Recreational activities which may hinder your recovery
• Sporting activities which would place your recovery at risk
• Secondary occupations
• Any other activity which may inhibit your recovery in any way

Medical appointments

8 You should endeavour to arrange hospital, medical and dental appointments outside your normal working hours or attempt to make appointments at the beginning or end of the working day, to minimise disruption. However, we recognise that this is not always possible, particularly when the need for urgent treatment arises. Leave with pay can be granted at management discretion to allow you to attend medical appointments at hospital. Where your appointments will entail a regular course of treatment, you will be expected to work alternative hours or take the time off as part of your annual leave entitlement. You will need to produce proof of appointments to your manager before taking time off in these circumstances.

I Answer these questions. Tick ✓ one of the boxes.

32 It's 11.30am. Latif is due to start work at 2pm, but he isn't feeling well. When should he get in touch with the store to let them know he's not going in?

a 11.30am ☐
b just after 2pm ☐
c just before 2pm ☐

33 How can he let the store know he's not going in?

a phone them ☐
b text them ☐
c email them ☐

34 Latif shares a flat with his brother and three friends. Who can contact the store?

a only Latif himself ☐
b Latif or his brother ☐
c Latif, his brother or one of his friends ☐

35 If Latif wants to get sick pay, what is the very latest time the store must be told that he won't be at work?

a 1pm ☐
b 2pm ☐
c 3pm ☐

36 What should Latif do if he is off work for three days?

a ask his manager for an interview ☐
b get a medical certificate from his doctor ☐
c complete a form about his absence from work ☐

J Replace the expressions in *italics* with your own words.

37 paragraph 3: *In the event of circumstances not permitting you to* report as noted,

----

38 paragraph 4: *Upon your return*, we will require self-certification

----

39 paragraph 5: *In cases of sickness*, this may mean that you will have to provide

----

40 paragraph 6: *you may be requested to* attend absence review meetings

----

41 paragraph 7: *During a period of sickness absence*, you are expected

----

42 paragraph 7: to act responsibly *in light of* any medical advice given

----

K Latif is telling one of his colleagues about the store's policy in connection with medical appointments. Complete what he says in your own words.

43 If you need to go to the dentist's, ----------------------------

----

44 If you have to have an appointment during the working day, ---

----

45 If you have lots of hospital appointments,

L You are going to read the entry in a book about the word OK. Read the first paragraph on the right and answer this question.

46 What do you think the next paragraph is going to be about? Tick ✓ one of the boxes.
a the worldwide use of OK ☐
b the meaning of OK ☐
c the origin of OK ☐

M Now read the first parts of paragraphs 2 and 3 of the section. (Notice how a colon is used here to introduce a list.) What is the topic of each paragraph? Choose from these options. Write the numbers 2 and 3 in two of the boxes.

47 and 48
a similar words and sounds to OK in other languages ☐
b place names which sound like OK ☐
c people's names beginning with OK ☐
d abbreviations to OK ☐

N Which paragraphs do these sentences belong to? Match the four sentences below with the two paragraphs. Write the numbers in the boxes.

49 A particularly persistent and long-standing theory says that President Andrew Jackson used to write OK to abbreviate the illiterate 'ole korrek' on documents, a grievous calumny on a well-educated man. ☐

50 Many African-Americans would be delighted to have it proved that OK is actually from an African language brought to America by slaves, but the evidence is against them, as we shall shortly learn. ☐

51 Such accidentally coincidental forms across languages are surprisingly common and all of these are quite certainly false. ☐

52 None of these theories can be supported with documented proof. ☐

OK

1   This is without doubt the best-known and widest-travelled Americanism, used and recognized everywhere even by people who hardly know another word of English. Running in parallel with its popularity have been many attempts to explain where it came from – amateur etymologists have been obsessed with *OK* and theories have bred unchecked for the past 150 years.

2   Suggestions abound of introductions from another language: from the Choctaw-Chickasaw *okah* meaning 'it is indeed'; from Greek *olla kalla*, 'all good'; from a mishearing of the Scots *och aye!* (or perhaps Ulster Scots *Ough aye!*), 'yes indeed'; from West African languages like Mandingo (*O ke*, 'certainly') or Wolof (*waw kay*, 'yes indeed'); from Finnish oikea, 'correct, exact'; from French *au quais*, 'at the quay' (supposedly stencilled on Puerto Rican rum specially selected for export, or a place of assignation for French sailors in the Caribbean); or from French *Aux Cayes* (a port in Haiti famous for its superior rum).

3   Some other theories I've seen mentioned: it comes from *Old Keokuk*, the name of a Native American Fox chief; from German *Oberst Kommandant*, 'Colonel in Command', because some German officer fought on the colonists' side in the American Revolution (names such as General Schliessen or Baron von Steuben are mentioned but cannot be linked to real individuals); from the name of a freight agent, *Obadiah Kelly*, whose initials often appeared on bills on lading; an abbreviation for *Open Key*, popularized by early telegraphers; or from the initials of *Orrin Kendall* biscuits supplied to the Union Army during the Civil War.

0 Read paragraph 4. Match the sentences with their functions. Write the numbers in the boxes.

53 sentence ☐ leads into the next paragraph

54 sentence ☐ refers back to the previous paragraph

55 sentence ☐ introduces the topic of the rest of the extract

P Which is the topic sentence in paragraph 5? Circle the correct number.

56 sentence 1   sentence 2   sentence 3

Q Which of these sentence parts make up the main point of paragraph 6? Write two letters in the boxes.

57 and 58 ☐ ☐

a Professor Read traced the earliest recorded use of *OK* to the Boston Morning Post of 23 March 1839,

b in a report about a 'frolicsome group' called the Anti-Bell Ringing Society (the ABRS),

c which campaigned to get a law banning the ringing of dinner bells rescinded.

d It seems to have been short for 'oll korrect',

e a fanciful way of writing 'all correct' that was itself part of another popular craze of the time for misspellings as a humorous device which echoes the story about President Jackson from the previous decade.

R Which of these sentences best summarises the main points of paragraph 7? Write the letter in the box.

59 ☐

a In 1840, *OK* was used as part of the name of a club which supported President Martin Van Buren in his campaign for re-election; his nickname was Old Kinderhook.

b President Martin Van Buren was known as Old Kinderhook because his birthplace was Kinderhook; the abbreviation was used in his 1840 campaign for re-election.

c Martin Van Buren lost the 1840 presidential election to William Harrison, but the initial letters of his nickname lived on.

4   I could go on, but it would only strain your patience and fortitude as it would mine. The true story was researched by Professor Allen Walker Read in the 1960s. Let me give you the facts as he uncovered them through his assiduous reading of local newspapers.

5   He records that 'beginning in the summer of 1838, there developed in Boston a remarkable vogue of using abbreviations. It might well be called a craze.' He quotes many examples, including *RTBS*, 'Remains To Be Seen', *GTDHD*, 'Give the Devil His Due', *OFM*, 'Our First Men' (a satirical description of Boston's leading citizens) and *SP*, 'Small Potatoes' (for something considered to be of little importance).

6   Professor Read traced the earliest recorded use of *OK* to the Boston Morning Post of 23 March 1839, in a report about a 'frolicsome group' called the Anti-Bell Ringing Society (the ABRS), which campaigned to get a law banning the ringing of dinner bells rescinded. It seems to have been short for 'oll korrect', a fanciful way of writing 'all correct' that was itself part of another popular craze of the time for misspellings as a humorous device which echoes the story about President Jackson from the previous decade.

7   What ensured that this one example survived out of many in a hugely popular but short-lived fashion was that it was picked up by the Democrats in New York. They created a body called the Democratic OK Club to support their candidate, Martin Van Buren, who was standing for re-election in the 1840 presidential election against William Henry Harrison. OK here actually stood for 'Old Kinderhook', Van Buren's nickname, taken from Kinderhook, his birthplace near Albany in New York State. The abbreviation became widely used during the campaign and survived Van Buren's losing the election.

8   However, its origins quickly became lost, as anything linked to yesterday's news usually does. Many earnest investigators have since tried to resolve the issue. Despite the fact that we have known the true story for the past forty years, people still keep coming up with ingenious but mistaken theories.

S Which sentence in the final paragraph (paragraph 8) links the ending of the section to the first paragraph? (You will need to read the first paragraph again.) Write the sentence number (1, 2 or 3) in the box.

60 ☐

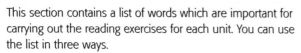

Appendix 1
Useful language

This section contains a list of words which are important for carrying out the reading exercises for each unit. You can use the list in three ways.

1 You can look at the list before you begin the unit and make sure that you understand the meaning of the words by looking them up in a dictionary.
2 You can look at the list before you begin the unit, but try and work out the meaning of the words when you meet them in the unit.
3 You can look at the list when you have completed the unit and check that you understand the words.

When you start using the book, you may prefer to use the list in the first way. However, you will find each word in one of the texts, and the context – the words around the unknown word – will help you to work out its meaning. As you develop your reading skills, you will probably realize that it is not necessary to look at the list before you begin the unit. You may already know some of the words; you will be able to work out others from the text or the task.

Each list is a record of the vocabulary of the unit. You can use it as a checklist when you have completed the unit. There is space after each word to write a translation in your own language or an English expression using the word. Mark each word that you understand and can use with a highlighter pen.

There is also space below the wordlist for you to write other words from the unit which are important to you. Look at *Appendix 3* for ideas on what to record for each word.

Unit 1
Reading A
receipt *noun* --
refund *noun* --
exchange *noun* --
purchase *noun* --
seal intact *expression* --
original packaging *noun* --

Reading B
redemption *noun* --
nominate *verb* --
convict *verb* --
sentence *noun* --
twist in the tail *expression* --

Unit **2**

Reading A
(health) hazard *noun* ....
pitfall *noun* ....
ailment *noun* ....
deep vein thrombosis *noun* ....
stationary *adjective* ....
callisthenics *noun* ....
predisposed *adjective* ....
penetrate *verb* ....
mole *noun* ....
benign *adjective* ....
fatal *adjective* ....
antivenin *noun* ....
life-threatening *adjective* ....
liberal (application) *adjective* ....
repellent *noun* ....
....
....
....

Reading B
blood clot *noun* ....
stopover *noun* ....
dehydration *noun* ....
immobility *noun* ....
sluggish *adjective* ....
circulation *noun* ....
circulatory (problems) *adjective* ....
thigh *noun* ....
right angle *noun* ....
calf *noun* ....
parallel *adjective* ....
hip-width *adjective* ....
bottom *noun* ....
....
....
....

Unit **3**

Reading A
disruption *noun* ....
divert *verb* ....
medical emergency *noun* ....
....
....
....

Reading B
insurance *noun* ....
cover *noun* ....
policy *noun* ....
claim *noun* ....
cancellation *noun* ....
excess *noun / adjective* ....
abandonment *noun* ....
written confirmation *noun* ....
....
....
....

Unit **4**

Reading A
victim *noun* ....
crime prevention *noun* ....
neighbourhood *noun* ....
....
....
....

Reading B
property *noun* ....
burglar *noun* ....
be/get burgled *verb* ....
break-in *noun* ....
secure *adjective* ....
....
....
....

Unit 5

Reading A

donated *adjective* _____

christening gown *noun* _____

constructed *adjective* _____

technique *noun* _____

style *noun* _____

insight *noun* _____

Renaissance *adjective* _____

come to fruition *expression* _____

ceramics *noun* _____

Baroque *adjective* _____

_____

_____

_____

Reading B

blazing (images) *adjective* _____

housing (paintings) *adjective* _____

_____

_____

_____

Unit 6

Reading A

conquer *verb* _____

impact *noun* _____

catch on *verb* _____

correspondent *noun* _____

compulsive *adjective* _____

(complex) ramifications *noun* _____

(subtle) strategies *noun* _____

rule supreme *expression* _____

_____

_____

_____

Reading B

stimulating *adjective* _____

chew over *verb* _____

meditation *noun* _____

thrash out *verb* _____

shake loose *expression* _____

smug *adjective* _____

distraction *noun* _____

_____

_____

_____

Unit 7

Reading A

quote *noun & verb* _____

shipment *noun* _____

plant *noun* _____

_____

_____

_____

Reading B

specifications *noun* _____

_____

_____

_____

Unit 8

Reading A

Personnel Manager *noun* _____

pave the way *expression* _____

(general) conduct *noun* _____

prerequisite *noun* _____

conservative (option) *adjective* _____

posture *noun* _____

clam up *verb* _____

authority *noun* _____

arrogance *noun* _____

negotiation *noun* _____

_____

_____

_____

Reading B

impromptu *adjective* _____

achievement *noun* _____

straightforward *adjective* _____

in your stride *expression* _____

technical proficiency *collocation* _____

outcome *noun* _____

_____

_____

_____

Unit**9**

Reading A

holiday entitlement *noun* _____
start of employment *noun* _____
end of the financial year *noun* _____
mutual agreement *noun* _____
annual leave *noun* _____
leave year *noun* _____
statutory days *noun* _____
floating day *noun* _____
time off in lieu *noun* _____
_____
_____
_____

Reading B

trade union representatives *noun* _____
mortgage *noun* _____
loan facility *noun* _____
line manager *noun* _____
_____
_____
_____

Unit**10**

Reading A

flexible *adjective* _____
guarantee *verb* _____
clock in/out *verb* _____
credit (margin) *noun* _____
debit (margin) *noun* _____
accounting period *noun* _____
into debt *collocation* _____
congestion *noun* _____
absenteeism *noun* _____
fatigue *noun* _____
morale *noun* _____
_____
_____
_____

Reading B

attendance (management systems / records / data / details) *noun* _____
incentive *noun* _____
(missed) clocking *noun* _____
password (clearance / protected) *noun* _____
_____
_____
_____

Unit**11**

Reading A

Colleague Council (meeting / member) *noun* _____
memo *noun* _____
minutes *noun* _____
feedback *noun* _____
feed back (on) *verb* _____
call barring *noun* _____
lease *noun* _____
financial hardship *noun* _____
ad-hoc usage *noun* _____
non-professional (courses) *adjective* _____
in-house (courses) *adjective* _____
apologies *noun* _____
_____
_____
_____

Reading B

feasibility *noun* _____
implementation *noun* _____
participant *noun* _____
enrolment *noun* _____
_____
_____
_____

Unit**12**

Reading A

scholarships *noun* _____
particular (departments / country / course) *adjective*
_____
recognize *verb* _____
entry requirements *noun* _____
semester (system) *noun* _____
(future) profession *noun* _____
_____
_____
_____

Reading B

(federally) regulate *verb* _____
_____
_____
_____

Unit 13
Reading A
obstacle *noun* _____
percentage gain *expression* _____
vocalizing *noun* _____
perceptible (movement) *adjective* _____
appreciation *noun* _____
(be) bound to *expression* _____
at random *expression* _____
_____
_____
_____

Reading B
grasp *verb* _____
skeleton outline *noun* _____
justify *verb* _____
(the very) essence *noun* _____
a doubtful necessity *expression* _____
_____
_____
_____

Unit 14
Reading A
contemporary *adjective* _____
domestic (economy) *adjective* _____
_____
_____
_____

Reading B
federally *adverb* _____
mandate *verb* _____
(be) subject to *expression* _____
overtime *noun* _____
overwhelm *verb* _____
assembly line *noun* _____
downsize *verb* _____
(personal) consumption *noun* _____
mortgage *noun* _____
prove your worth *collocation* _____
retain *verb* _____
layoff *noun* _____
commute *noun/verb* _____
labor force *noun* _____
in motion *expression* _____
counterpart *noun* _____
(work) ethic *noun* _____
_____
_____
_____

Unit 15
Reading A
(conservative / radical) estimate *noun* _____
examination board *noun* _____
iceberg *noun* _____
(massive) influx *noun* _____
(significant) impact *noun* _____
(enormous) motivation *noun* _____
retrieval system *noun* _____
_____
_____
_____

Reading B
(majority / external) influence *noun* _____
trend *noun* _____
loan word *noun* _____
mistletoe *noun* _____
prestige connotations *noun* _____
_____
_____
_____

Unit 16
Reading A
passage *noun* _____
paraphrase *verb* _____
_____
_____
_____

Appendix 2
Learning tips

Each unit of this book contains one *Learning tip*. However, this does not mean that this *Learning tip* is useful in only that particular unit. Most *Learning tips* can be used in several different units. Here are all the *Learning tips* in the book. Each one is under its unit heading and you will also find a list of the types of text you read in that unit.

When you have completed a unit, decide which text you used the *Learning tip* with (this could be more than one text type). In addition, look at the other *Learning tips* and decide if you also used any of those tips in the unit you have just finished. Make a note of the unit name and number and the text type on the empty lines. In this way, you can keep a record of the reading strategies that you are developing.

Unit 1 I'll take it!

Learning tip

We use a technique called scanning when we search a text for a particular word or words. This involves looking quickly at the text without considering the meaning. Once we have found what we are looking for, we may then read the text around the word(s).

A receipt ☐
   guarantee ☐
B DVD cover ☐

Which other units have you used this *Learning tip* in?

Unit 2 Take care of yourself

Learning tip

When we read a text for the first time, we often use a technique known as *skimming* – looking over a text rapidly to get a general impression. This does not remove the need for careful reading later, but it allows us to select parts of the text that are worth re-reading. We then read these particular phrases, sentences or sections more carefully in order to understand the details. Remember that there are different ways in which we can read a text, and the technique we use depends on the type of text and our reason for reading.

A guidebook ☐
B leaflet ☐
   magazine ☐

Which other units have you used this *Learning tip* in?

Unit3 Our flight's delayed

Learning tip

Texts may often contain words that you have not met before. (This can also happen in your own language.) Try not to use your dictionary every time you come across a new word. The word might not be important in terms of extracting the message from the text – so you can ignore it. Alternatively, you may be able to work out its meaning from related words or from the context – the words around it. Try to get into the habit of only using the dictionary as a last resort – or to check that you guessed the meaning correctly.

A ticket ☐
  letter ☐
B insurance policy ☐

Which other units have you used this *Learning tip* in?

Unit4 I've been burgled

Learning tip

Punctuation is used in writing to divide up groups of words and make them easier to read. When speaking, you vary the speed and loudness of the words and add pauses. In writing, punctuation marks show these variations. Each punctuation mark is used for its own particular purpose; they can help you to predict what is coming next in a text. Paying attention to punctuation can help you to read more efficiently.

A letter ☐
B brochure ☐

Which other units have you used this *Learning tip* in?

Unit5 Picasso's birthplace

Learning tip

Writers do not always state facts directly, so readers have to infer them (work them out) for themselves using the clues available. Think about the words you are reading, and ask yourself 'So, what does this tell me?'.

A guidebook ☐
B leaflet ☐

Which other units have you used this *Learning tip* in?

Unit6 Love it or loathe it!

Learning tip

Our purpose in reading a text is to understand the writer's message. This means understanding the words the writer uses and also understanding what the writer wants to do with these words. This could be presenting facts, describing a series of events, giving an opinion. Understanding a text requires us to work out the function of each sentence.

A newspaper article ☐
B newspaper article ☐

Which other units have you used this *Learning tip* in?

Unit 7 Import, export!

Learning tip

Understanding a text is a two-way process between writer and reader. It works best when the message is written clearly. Sometimes the reader lacks background knowledge of the subject, so the writer's message is not entirely clear. The reader may need to do some further reading or ask someone for clarification.

A emails ☐
B emails ☐

Which other units have you used this *Learning tip* in?

Unit 8 I've got an interview

Learning tip

Before you start reading a text in English, ask yourself what you already know about the topic of the text – or what you would do in the situation that it describes. Focusing your thoughts will help you to predict the content of the text and allow you to relate what you read to your own ideas and experiences.

A leaflet ☐
B leaflet ☐

Which other units have you used this *Learning tip* in?

Unit 9 What's your new job like?

Learning tip

We use neutral language in most of our everyday communication. However, sometimes we have to read texts written in formal language – legal documents, in particular. The language is often impersonal: the third person and the passive are used; there are no contractions; sentences are long and complicated; and there are lots of nouns and noun phrases. Formal language is unlike the spoken language that we are used to. You can make sure you have understood a formal text by putting it into less formal everyday language. This means rephrasing the sentences rather than simply replacing individual words with less formal alternatives.

A terms and conditions ☐
B letter ☐

Which other units have you used this *Learning tip* in?

Unit 10 I've got Thursday off

Learning tip

When the register of a text is impersonal and technical, long words are more commonly used. Nouns are often used together in groups, with one noun describing another noun. (The noun *holiday* describes the noun *pay* in *holiday pay*, for example.) You will need to be able to recognize such groups and to work out which is the main noun within the group (it is usually the last one). This will help you to understand the structure of the sentence and the text.

A webpage ☐
B webpage ☐

Which other units have you used this *Learning tip* in?

Appendix 2 Learning tips

Unit 11 I've read the minutes

Learning tip

Always look at the title and headings before you start reading a text. This is because they help you to understand what is and what is not in a text. You will usually find headings in business correspondence – letters, minutes, email, reports – because the aim is for maximum clarity.

A   memo ☐
     minutes ☐
     email ☐
B   email ☐
     report ☐

Which other units have you used this *Learning tip* in?

Unit 12 The course is in English

Learning tip

Headings, italics and bold indicate what type of information you are going to find in a text. Specific signalling words or phrases, such as *However, Therefore, Furthermore*, can help you to predict what is coming next in the text. When the words are at the beginning of a sentence, they link the new sentence to the previous one. Words and phrases like *because, so, in order to* are usually found in the middle of a sentence (although they can be at the beginning) and they link the two parts of that sentence. Recognizing and understanding such words and phrases can help you to read more efficiently. They also help you to understand the structure of the text.

A   handbook ☐
B   handbook ☐
     webpage ☐

Which other units have you used this *Learning tip* in?

Unit 13 Read faster!

Learning tip

When you are reading, try not to let your eyes regress – do not stop and re-read words you have just read. Keep on going forwards rather than going back. If you are unsure of something, the meaning may become clear from the rest of the sentence/paragraph/text. If the meaning is still unclear when you have finished reading, you can always return to this part of the text if you think that it is vital to comprehension.

A   coursebook ☐
B   coursebook ☐

Which other units have you used this *Learning tip* in?

Unit 14 I've chosen this topic

Learning tip

In the classroom, we are usually given the texts we need to read. Sometimes, however, we need to actually find the best extract within a book for our purposes. Use a mixture of skimming and scanning to find out if a book is suitable and likely to provide you with the information you are looking for; skim the blurb (back cover) to get an overall feel for the book; scan the Contents and the Index to find your topic; then go to the pages that are mentioned in the Index to find the entry (word from the Index) you are looking for; and skim the text around the word. Then decide how useful the text is for your task.

A   reference book blurb ☐
     reference book contents ☐
     reference book index ☐
B   reference book extracts ☐

Which other units have you used this *Learning tip* in?

Unit **15** English today

Learning tip

In general, a paragraph deals with a single topic – for example, an event, a description, or an idea. It usually – but not always – contains a topic sentence (one that sums up the main point of the paragraph). If you can identify the topic, the main point, and the minor or supporting points, then you have understood the organization of the paragraph. If you can identify how the author links one paragraph to the next, then you will see how the author's ideas hang together. This will make the text more accessible to you.

A reference book extracts ☐
B reference book extracts ☐

Which other units have you used this *Learning tip* in?

Unit **16** I need a good score

Learning tip

The IELTS Reading Sub-test is in three sections. There are three passages with a combined length of 2000–2750 words and a total of 40 questions. You have only one hour to answer the questions – there is quite a risk that you will run out of time. Your aim is not to understand the writer's message but to answer the questions. This is your purpose in reading and it should determine the way you read the text. Always have a question in mind when you read the text – and give yourself a reason for reading.

A exam preparation handbook ☐
B exam passage and tasks ☐

Which other units have you used this *Learning tip* in?

Appendix 3
Using a dictionary

What kind of dictionary should I use?

If possible, you should use two dictionaries: a good bilingual dictionary (in both your own language and with English translations) and a good monolingual dictionary (English words with English definitions). The dictionary which has translations in your own language is quicker and easier for you to understand. The dictionary with definitions in English, on the other hand, may give you more information about a word or phrase; in addition, it is a good idea for you to work in English as much as possible. The examples on these pages are from the *Cambridge Advanced Learner's Dictionary*.

What information can I find in a dictionary?

The most common reason for looking a word up in a dictionary is to find out its meaning. However, a dictionary can also give you a lot of other information about a word. The *Cambridge Advanced Learner's Dictionary*, for example, can give up to six types of information before the meaning of the word and three further types of information after it. These examples are all from Unit 1.

1 the headword

> The words at the beginning of entries are called 'headwords'. Usually they are black, but the most important words are blue.

> **engrossed** /ɪnˈgrəʊst/ ⑤ /-ˈgroʊst/ *adj* giving all your attention to something; absorbed: *She was so engrossed **by/in** the book that she forgot the cakes in the oven.* ○ *They were so engrossed **in/with** what they were doing that they didn't hear me come in.*

2 the pronunciation of the word

> These symbols show you how to say the word.

> **warranty** /ˈwɒr.ᵊn.ti/ ⑤ /ˈwɔːr.ᵊn.i/ *noun* [C] a written promise from a company to repair or replace a product that develops a fault within a fixed period of time, or to do a piece of work again if it is not satisfactory; a GUARANTEE: *The warranty **covers** the car mechanically for a year, with unlimited mileage.*

3 its part of speech

> This tells you what part of speech – noun, verb, adjective, etc. – a word is

> **unlikely** Ⓔ /ʌnˈlaɪ.kli/ *adj* not LIKELY: [+ (**that**)] *It's pretty unlikely (that) they'll turn up now – it's nearly ten o'clock.* ○ *He seems an unlikely-looking policeman* (= He is not what I expect a policeman to look like).

4 any special grammatical features of the word

> **mishap** /ˈmɪs.hæp/ *noun* [C or U] bad luck, or an unlucky event or accident: *The parade was very well organised and passed without mishap.* ○ *A series of mishaps led to the nuclear power plant blowing up.*

5 irregular past tense forms, plural nouns, and comparatives/superlatives

> **keep** POSSESS **E** /kiːp/ *verb* [T] (**kept, kept**) **1** to have or continue to have in your possession: *Do you want this photograph back or can I keep it?*
> **2** to own and manage a small shop: *My uncle kept a little tobacconist's in Gloucester.*

6 whether the word is only used in British English (UK) or American English (US)

UK means that a word is only used in British English; *US* means that a word is used only in American English.

> **receipt** **A** /rɪˈsiːt/ *noun* [C] (*US ALSO* **sales slip**) a piece of paper which proves that money, goods or information have been received: *Make sure you are given a receipt **for** everything you buy.*

7 the meaning of the word

> **nickname** **A** /ˈnɪk.neɪm/ *noun* [C] an informal name for someone or something, especially a name which you are called by your friends or family, usually based on your proper name or your character: *We always use the nickname Beth for our daughter Elizabeth.* ○ *"Darwin" was the nickname he was given at high school, because of his interest in science.* **nickname** /ˈnɪk.neɪm/ *verb* [T + obj + noun]: *The campsite has been nicknamed 'tent city' by visiting reporters.*

The definition tells you what the word means.

8 example phrases or sentences

> **helpline** /ˈhelp.laɪn/ *noun* [C] a telephone service providing advice and comfort to worried or unhappy people: *A new helpline is now available for people trying to stop smoking.*

Examples (in *italics*) can show you how a word is used in a phrase/sentence.

9 other words this word goes with (collocations)

> **assistance** **I** /əˈsɪs.tᵊnts/ *noun* [U] help: *The company needs more **financial** assistance from the Government.* ○ *A £1 billion investment would be **of** considerable assistance to the railways.*

Words in **bold** in an example show you which words are often used together.

10 other words from the same family

> **extraordinary** **I** /ɪkˈstrɔː.dɪn.ᵊr.i/ US /-ˈstrɔːr.dᵊn.er-/ *adj* **1** very unusual, special, unexpected or strange: *He told the extraordinary story of his escape.* ○ *Her voice had an extraordinary hypnotic quality.* ○ *an extraordinary coincidence* **2 extraordinary meeting** a special meeting which happens between regular meetings

Words in the same family are often grouped together.

How should I use my dictionary?

1 At the top of each page in the *Cambridge Advanced Learner's Dictionary*, there is a word in **bold** black type. The word in the top left corner of the left page is the first word on this page; the word in the top right corner of the right page is the last word on this page. If you are looking for the word **amass**, it will be between the two words **amanuensis** and **amicable** (top right corner of the right page).

---

amanuensis
....

separate organizations do this: *The electricians' union is planning to amalgamate **with** the technicians' union.* ○ *The different offices will be amalgamated **as/into** employment advice centres.* **amalgamation** /ə,mæl.gə-'meɪ.ʃⁿn/ *noun* [C or U]: *The association was **formed by** the amalgamation of several regional environmental organizations.* ○ *The company began as an amalgamation of small family firms.*

amanuensis /ə,mæn.ju'ent.sɪs/ *noun* [C] (*plural* **amanuenses**) FORMAL a person whose job is to write down what another person says or to copy what another person has written

amass /ə'mæs/ *verb* [T] to get a large amount of something, especially money or information, by collecting it over a long period: *She has amassed a huge **fortune** from her novels.* ○ *Some of his colleagues envy the enormous **wealth** that he has amassed.*

---

2 Each time you look up a word, use a highlighter pen to mark the word in your dictionary. When you return to a page with a highlighter mark, look at the word quickly and check that you remember its meaning.

'guide ,dog *noun* [C] a dog that has been specially trained to help a blind person travel around safely: *guide dogs for the blind*

guideline ❶ /'gaɪd.laɪnz/ *noun* [usually pl] information intended to advise people on how something should be done or what something should be: *The EU has **issued** guidelines on appropriate levels of pay for part-time manual workers.*

the Guides *plural noun* an international organization for young women which encourages them to take part in different activities and to become responsible and independent ➔Compare **the Scouts**.

---

3 A word in your dictionary may not be exactly the same as its form in the text you are reading. This is because the word in the text may be: a plural form of a noun; a comparative or superlative form of an adjective; an irregular form of a verb or a verb ending in *-s, -ed, -ing*, e.g. *dying*.

---

die STOP LIVING **Ⓔ** /daɪ/ *verb* [I] (**dying, died, died**) **1** to stop living or existing, either suddenly or slowly: *Twelve people died in the accident.* ○ *She died **of/from** hunger/* **2 die a natural/violent, etc. death** to die naturally, violently, etc: *He died a violent death.*

---

4 Some words in your dictionary may have more than one headword because they have several meanings. In this case, there are guide words to help you find the meaning you are looking for. Usually the most common meaning appears first, after the headword in blue. The first meaning in the dictionary is not always the one you want. Read through the different meanings and decide which one is correct in this context.

---

custom TRADITION **❶** /'kʌs.təm/ *noun* [C or U] a way of behaving or a belief which has been established for a long time: *a local/ancient custom* ○ [+ to infinitive] *In my country, it's **the** custom **(for** women) to get married in white.* **customary** /'kʌs.tə.mⁿr.i/ ⑤ /-mer-/ *adj*: [+ to infinitive] *In my village, **it** is customary **for** a girl **to** take her mother's name.*

custom USUAL ACTIVITY /'kʌs.təm/ *noun* [S] something you usually do: *He left the house at nine exactly, **as is** his custom.*
customary /'kʌs.tə.mⁿr.i/ ⑤ /-mer-/ *adj*: *She's not her customary* (= usual) *cheerful self today.* **customarily** /kʌs.tə'mer.ɪ.li/ *adv*

custom TRADE /'kʌs.təm/ *noun* [U] the support given to a business, especially a shop, by the people who buy things or services from it: *Most of our custom comes from tourists nowadays.* ○ *If we don't give good service, people will **take** their custom **elsewhere**.*

5 In other cases, other smaller differences in meaning of a noun/verb/adjective etc. appear under one headword. Usually the most common meaning appears first. However, the first meaning in the dictionary is not always the one you want. Read through the different meanings and decide which one is correct in this context.

> **circumstance** ❶ /'sɜː.kəm.stɑːn*ts*/ ⑩ /'sɝː.kəm.stæn*ts*/ *noun* **1** [**C** usually plural] a fact or event that makes a situation the way it is: *I think she coped very well **under the circumstances**.* ○ *Obviously we can't deal with the problem until we know all the circumstances.* ○ *She died **in suspicious** circumstances.* ○ *We oppose capital punishment **in/under any** circumstances.* ○ ***Under no** circumstances should you (= You must not) approach the man.* ○ *The meeting has been cancelled **due to** circumstances **beyond our control**.* **2** [**U**] *FORMAL* events that change your life, over which you have no control: *They were victims of circumstance.* ○ *We were obliged to go by force of circumstance.* **3 circumstances** how much money someone has: *Grants are available depending on your circumstances.* ○ *By now she was alone and living **in** reduced circumstances (= with little money).*

6 When a word can be used as different parts of speech – for example, a noun and a verb – and the meanings are related, they both appear under the same headword. The part of speech of the unknown word should be clear from the context (the words around it). Note that the pronunciation may differ for each part of speech.

> **refund** /'riː.fʌnd/ *noun* [**C**] an amount of money that is given back to you, especially because you are not happy with a product or service that you have bought: *I took the radio back to the shop and asked for/demanded/got/ was given a refund.*
> **refund** /ˌrɪˈfʌnd/ *verb* [**T**] to give someone a refund: *When I went on business to Peru, the office refunded my expenses.* ○ [+ two objects] *The holiday was cancelled so the travel agency had to refund everybody the price of the tickets.* **refundable** /ˌriːˈfʌn.də.bl̩/ *adj*

7 Dictionaries are particularly helpful with the meaning of phrasal verbs and idioms since their meaning is different from the meaning of the separate parts. You will find phrasal verbs, idioms and other expressions after all the other definitions of the word.

When should I use my dictionary?

A dictionary is very useful when you are learning a foreign language. However, when you are reading, do not use your dictionary too much. Using your dictionary will interrupt your reading and slow you down. In your own language, you don't always understand the meaning of every word; it is not necessary to understand everything in English either.

1 When you see an English word that you don't know, first try to guess the meaning of the word from its context (the words around it). You may find another word with a similar meaning, a word which means the opposite, or some words which actually explain the unknown word. Only use your dictionary to check your guess.

2 The only other time you should look a word up in your dictionary is if there are no clues in the text and you are sure the unknown word is important.

Answer key

Get ready to read

○ a S b C c C d S
○ *Your own answers.*

A

1. a He bought the DVD player on September 24th.
   b It cost £69.99.
   c He should keep his receipt because he will need it if he wants a refund or an exchange.

2. Section 1 – *exchange*: lines 2 and 12; *refund*: lines 2 and 12
   Section 2 – *exchange*: line 3 (also *exchanged*: line 18); *refund*: lines 4 and 6 (also *refunded*: line 19)
   Section 3 – *refund*: line 7

3. a He could get an exchange or a refund if he changed his mind about the DVD player.
   b He would have to change his mind within seven days of buying it.
   c He would have to return the DVD player unopened (with any seal intact) and unused.

4. a He could get an exchange or a refund if the DVD player developed a fault.
   b He could get an exchange or a refund within 28 days of buying it.
   c If he wanted a refund, he would have to return the DVD player in 'as new' condition. Presumably if he wanted an exchange, he wouldn't need to return it 'as new'.

Focus on the negative prefix *-un* with participles

1. The product must be
   • Unopened (with any seal intact)
   • Unused
2. b unaided c unemployed d uncommitted
   e unspoken f uncut

5. a This section mentions *refund* because it is talking about money you would get if you saw a cheaper identical DVD player in a shop within 10 miles. An exchange would not be appropriate here.
   b If Roberto saw a cheaper identical DVD player, he could get a refund of the price difference plus another 10% of the difference.
   c He could get a refund within seven days of buying it.

6. a £11 – the difference of £10 + 10% of £10 (£1)
   b nothing – more than seven days after his purchase
   c nothing – too far from the shop where he bought his DVD player
   d nothing – the Price Promise does not apply to Internet purchases.

7. *Your own answer. Possible answer:*
   I try to keep receipts, but sometimes I lose them. I needed a reciept when I decided to change a shirt I didn't want.

B

1. *See Exercise 2 for the answers.*
2. b (The other film in Exercise 1 is *The Green Mile*.)
3.

City Banker, Andy Dufresne (Tim Robbins), arrived at Shawshank Prison in 1947, <u>convicted of two brutal murders. He received a double life sentence.</u>
He discovers that when they send you to Shawshank State Prison for life … that is exactly what they take.
Within the confines of Shawshank, Andy <u>forms an unlikely friendship with the prison "fixer" Red</u> (Morgan Freeman). <u>He also becomes popular with the warden and the prison's guards, as Andy is able to use his banking experience to help the corrupt officials amass personal fortunes.</u>

4. a Right ✓: *The Shawshank Redemption* was released in 1994.
   b Right ✓: *The Shawshank Redemption* is 137 minutes long.
   c Right ✓: one of the actors got a nomination for Best Actor. (This was Morgan Freeman.)
   d Right ✓: the director's name was Frank Darabont. (*The Shawshank Redemption* was his first film.)
   e Wrong ✗: Tim Robbins played the main character and Morgan Freeman played 'Red'. (Tom Hanks played the prison guard in *The Green Mile*.)
   f Right ✓: *The Shawshank Redemption* is based on a short novel by Stephen King. (*The Green Mile* is also based on a Stephen King story.)

5. Most people will probably agree that Andy is likely to be saved because he is the main character.

6. *Your own answer. Possible answer:*
   I might see this film, but I'm not very keen on crime and prison dramas.

7. *Your own answer. Possible answer:*
   This person wasn't very keen on *The Shawshank Redemption* when she started watching it, but now she thinks it is the best movie ever made. This is a very strong recommendation!

Unit 2

Get ready to read

Your own answers.

A

1 No. New Zealand is a safe country to visit.
2 No, reading the paragraphs shouldn't change your answer in any way.
3 2 DVT 3 sun 4 wildlife
   5 mosquitoes and sandflies (insects)

> **Focus on colloquial language**
>
> 1 b booze c slap on d nasties e critter f beasts
> 2 b children c pounds d I haven't got any money.
>   e clever f friend

4/5

paragraph	hazard	precautions	remedies
2	DVT	move about in the plane perform stationary callisthenics; drink plenty of water; limit the amount of booze you consume	
3	sun	stay out of the sun as much as possible between 11 am and 3 pm; always slap on plenty of sunblock	
4	wildlife		antivenin is available for those who are bitten by the female katipo spider
5	mosquitoes and sandflies	use repellent	

6 *Your own answer. Possible answer:*
The most important piece of advice is in the introduction: don't forget to take precautions and don't underestimate the power of nature.

B

1 a 2, 4, 5, 6
   b *Your own answer. Possible answer:*
      I think sections 2, 4 and 6 will be the most useful.

3 DVT is a serious condition where blood clots develop in the deep veins of the legs.
4 precautions
5 Yes – Exercise 2 is similar to the second exercise (third bullet point) in the leaflet.

Unit 3

Get ready to read

- A flight might by delayed for any of the five reasons.
- *Your own answer. Possible answer:*
  I was going to Chile with Lufthansa, so I had to fly to Frankfurt and then get the plane to Santiago. Unfortunately, the plane had engine trouble and we had to spend the night in a hotel in Frankfurt.
- a curtail
  b cancel
  c postpone
- *Your own answer. Possible answer:*
  I didn't exactly cancel the holiday. My best friend and I planned to go on holiday together, but we had an argument a couple of days before we were going to leave. So I just didn't go on holiday. I don't know if she went – we haven't spoken since then.

A

1 a Cape Town b 27th August c 19.20 d BA
2 a The letter is to BA customers, i.e. passengers on flight 0059. It's from the British Airways Customer Service Duty Manager.
   b The plane didn't reach its destination because there was a medical emergency onboard, i.e. someone on the plane was seriously ill and needed medical attention.
   c The plane was at Heathrow – its departure point – when the letter was handed out.
3 *Your own answer. Possible answer:*
   I imagine the cabin crew can only work a certain number of hours, e.g. a maximum of 12. Because the plane had to return to Barcelona (and also probably spent time using up some of its fuel in order to land there), it would not be able to reach its destination within this period of time. In addition, the crew would have reached their maximum number of flying hours.
4 a Your new departure time will be 18:00 on 28th August, arriving in Cape Town at 06:40 on 29th August.

   b We have arranged accommodation for you at the Renaissance Hotel.

   c We suggest that you take your hold luggage with you when you go to the hotel.

   d For your transport to the hotel, you will need to make your way to bus stop 15. This is located outside the main Terminal building.

5 a The airline has also paid for a three-minute telephone call for either each person or each group of people (the letter doesn't make this clear).

b They have arranged this so that passengers can warn their friends, family, etc. in South Africa of the delay and their new arrival time.

6 a The prefix *dis* is negative (*dislike, disagree, dishonest*). A *disruption* is when a system, process or event is prevented from continuing as usual or as expected.

b *BA0059* and *aircraft* – refer to the *service*. The dictionary definition of *service* is 'the operation of a system'.

c The *lobby* is the room in a hotel into which the main entrance door opens.

d The prefix *in* is negative. This is the negative form of the noun *convenience* – a related word is the adjective *convenient*. The dictionary definition of *inconvenience* is 'a state or example of problems or trouble, which often causes a delay or loss of comfort'.

e You might also feel annoyed, or even angry. *Frustration* is related to the verb *frustrate* which means 'to prevent the plans or efforts of someone or something from being achieved'.

f *Brief* is the opposite of *long* – it means 'lasting only a short time'.

7 none of the words

Class bonus

Your own answers. Possible answers:
Some of the passengers might arrive too late for meetings, appointments, etc. Others, who were only going for a short visit, might decide not to go at all.
There would be no plane in Cape Town on the morning of the 28th. The passengers who were waiting in Cape Town and who should have flown to Heathrow on the 28th would need accommodation until the 29th (their rescheduled flight time). In addition, either the airline would need to find a change of crew – or the original crew would have to fly to Cape Town one day later than scheduled – and this would affect people's work schedules later in the week.

B

1 c

2 Travel delay and Abandonment

3 a They might be able to claim £20 each – for the first full 12 hours they will be delayed. They could claim an extra £10 if the plane left 24 hours later than scheduled.

b No, their cause of delay – medical emergency – isn't mentioned as one of the causes that is covered.

4 a They would need to have written confirmation from the airline, stating the period and the reason for the delay.

b They have got a letter from the airline (the letter on page 19).

c *Your own answer. Possible answer:*
I don't think they'll make a claim. It's not really worth the effort.

Focus on ways of travelling

1 a trip b crossing c flight d journey
2 a journey b flight c trip d crossing
3 a tour b excursion c ride d cruise

5 They should be able to claim up to the amount under the cancellation section of the policy (£5,000) less £50 excess, i.e. £4,500.

6 Pierre and Sophie abandoned their plan to make a claim because this part of the policy stresses that cover is only provided for three specific reasons – and medical emergency is not one of these.

Unit 4

Get ready to read

o

		crime	criminal	verb
a	stealing something from a shop	shoplifting	shoplifter	shoplift
b	stealing from a person or a place	robbery	robber	rob
c	stealing from someone's pocket	pickpocketing	pickpocket	pickpocket
d	taking something illegally into another country	smuggling	smuggler	smuggle
e	stealing from someone's home	burglary	burglar	burgle
f	attacking someone and stealing from them in a public place	mugging	mugger	mug

g *Your own answers. Possible answers*:

	crime	criminal	verb
killing someone	murder	murderer	murder
taking control of an aeroplane during a flight by force	hijack	hijacker	hijack
making an illegal copy of something	forgery	forger	forge
setting fire to something intentionally	arson	arsonist	*no verb*
attacking someone	assault	assailant	assault
killing someone important or famous	assassination	assassin	assassinate
taking someone away by force, saying you will only bring them back if someone gives money	kidnap	kidnapper	kidnap

A

1 The letter is from the police.
2 a 3   b 4   c 2   d 1
3 a to end a sentence
   b to add extra information, to separate items in a list
   c to introduce a name/number
   d to separate two parts of a sentence
   e to add extra information
   f to mark the beginning and end of the title

Focus on the passive

1 b will be contacted
   c has been identified
   d will be held
   e are analysed
   f will be reopened
2 b We will contact you
   c If we have identified no one
   d we will hold your report
   e we (constantly) analyse such crimes
   f we will reopen your case

---

5 a 2 b 3 c 5 d 4 e 6 f 1
6 *Your own answer. Possible answer*:
   I have never been burgled, but a friend of mine has been burgled twice. Her computer, TV and DVD player were all stolen.

B

1 *Your own answers. Possible answers*:
   a The aim of the brochure is to give you advice on how to 'beat the burglar', i.e. on how to prevent burglaries in the home.
   b The first two parts will tell you to close and lock windows and doors. They will also tell you which types of windows and doors give you the best protection against burglars. The third part could be about lighting, e.g. leaving lights on when you go out, having lights in the street/garden, etc. It might also mention burglar alarms. (As well as mentioning all of these things, this part of the brochure mentions spare keys, side passages, garages and sheds, and gates and fences.) You are going to read the final part of the leaflet in this section of the unit.
2 *See Exercise 3 for the answers.*
3 The sections *Be a good neighbout* and *Crime and preventation advice* are about the prevention of crime. Three of the sections are about what precautions you can take (right now – in *Postcode your property* and *Insurance*, and after a burglary – in *If you are burgled*) and one is related to security rather than burglary (*Smoke detector*).
4 a things that belong to someone
   b items, the object, valuable items, (stolen) goods
5
> Only use UV marking when other methods would reduce the value of the object – because the mark can fade.
> Take pictures of all valuable items like jewellery and silverware and write down the serial numbers of your TV, video, hi-fi, home computer and camera equipment, to help the police identify them should they be recovered. If you have many valuable items, fit a safe.
> Ask your local police station for 'postcoded property' stickers to display in the front and back windows of your house.
>
> **SMOKE DETECTORS**
> With all security, consideration must be given to the risk of fire and means of escape. Fit a smoke detector – a minimum of one per floor – installed to the manufacturer's instructions.
>
> **BE A GOOD NEIGHBOUR**
> If you see anyone acting suspiciously in your neighbourhood, call the police. There are now over 130,000 Neighbourhood Watch Schemes in this country – why not join one? Anyone can start up a Watch – call your police for details.
>
> **IF YOU ARE BURGLED**
> A secure home will reduce the chance of you getting burgled. But, if you get home and notice signs of a break-in:
> • Don't go in or call out – the intruder could still be inside.
> • Go to a neighbour's house to call the police.
>
> **CRIME PREVENTION ADVICE**
> All police forces have officers trained in crime prevention – contact your local station for advice.

6 The section *Insurance* doesn't tell you what to do.
   Your own answer. Possible answer:
   Take out insurance on your property.
7 *Your own answer. Possible answer*:
   I'm not sure that I will mark my property, but I might take pictures of all my valuable items. Neighbourhood Watch sounds like quite a good idea – we don't have anything like that in Italy.

Answer key

Get ready to read

- a Spain b Spain c France d France
- *Your own answer. Possible answer:*
  Picasso is the most famous painter there has ever been. His career had different periods when his painting style changed. He is best known for his Cubist pictures.

A

1 Yes, your friend recommends a visit to the museum she is talking about. She says opening hours are 'convenient' (a), it isn't expensive (c), you can see lots of paintings there (d), the museum is 'beautiful' (f) and the museum is 'very interesting' (h).

2 No, the Fundación Municipal Pablo Ruiz Picasso is not the museum your friend was talking about. Some of the things she said in Exercise 1 could be true for this museum, e.g. sentences b, g, h but the other sentences are either untrue, e.g. sentences a, c, d, e or unlikely to be true, e.g. sentence f.

3
> Situated in the historic Plaza de la Merced, the house where Picasso was born has been converted into a study centre about the life and works of the painter …

4 Yes, the Picasso Museum of Málaga is the museum your friend was talking about.

5

Picasso Museum Málaga

Palacio de Buenavista. San Agustin, 8
(Tues–Thurs 10 am–8 pm, Fri & Sat 10 am–9 pm, Sun 10 am–8 pm; (a) permanent collection €6, temporary collection €4.50, combined ticket for both €8; (c) www.museopicassomalaga.org)

The Picasso Museum of Málaga is currently displaying more than three hundred works which range through the painter's artistic career, as well as different techniques and styles, which enable the visitor to gain a great insight into his work. (h) The Picasso Museum is located in the Palacio de Buenavista, a building of great beauty featuring Andalucian Renaissance architecture, (e/f) which came to fruition thanks to donations from Christine and Bernard Ruiz Picasso, the artist's daughter-in-law and grandson. (g)

The permanent collection contains 204 works, including oils, etchings, drawings and ceramics, ranging from the 19th century up to 1972. (d) The best-known are 'Retrato de Paulo con gorro blanco', dedicated to the artist's first child, whose birth inspired his neoclassic style after the Cubist period, and 'Olga Kokhlova con mantilla', which is a portrait of his first wife wearing a Spanish mantilla (shawl), and which is considered to be one of his best works.

'The Picassos of Antibes' (until 11th June) This exhibition, on display for the first time in Spain, includes 73 works from the Musée Picasso Antibes (d) (Antibes, France) carried out by the artist after the Second World War.

The Buenavista Palace was declared a national monument in 1939 and is situated right in the historic centre of the city. Among the museum's facilities are a library, an auditorium, a document centre and a cafeteria. (b) The magnificent Mudejar artistry of the Palace, its Renaissance and Baroque ceilings and its fantastic view are more excellent reasons to visit the museum, which covers an overall area of 8,300 square metres. (e/f)

6 *Your own answers. Possible answers:*
  b *I looked around for a while* and then went to a nearby café to have something to eat.
  c *It didn't cost* anything to get in.
  d *You can see* works by Picasso and his father, and some personal items (including a christening gown).
  e *The building dates from* 1861.
  f *The building itself* used to be a house.
  g *Picasso's family have given* personal items.
  h *I learned a lot about* the childhood and the work of Picasso.

7 b The permanent collection of the Picasso Museum of Málaga contains works ranging from the 19th century up to 1972. This could be either the last year in which he painted or the year in which he died. He certainly didn't die before 1972.
  c In the Fundación Municipal Pablo Ruiz Picasso, you can see works both by Picasso and his father, José Ruiz Blasco.
  d Olga Kohklova does not sound like a traditional Spanish name. It is more typical of Eastern Europe, so it is likely that his first wife was not Spanish.
  e 'Retrato de Paulo con gorro blanco' is dedicated to the artist's first child, which means he had either another child or more children.
  f The 73 works from the Musée Picasso Antibes were carried out by the artist after the Second World War. Firstly, Antibes is in the south of France, and would be a wonderful place to display any works that had been done there. Secondly, the war ended in 1945. The fact that the Second World War is mentioned in the description suggests that the war had just finished when Picasso did the works.

8 *Your own answers. Possible answers:*
  I don't know for sure, but Christine could have been Paulo's wife – and Bernard their son. If so, then it seems that Paulo may have died.
  Olga was probably Paulo's mother.
  Perhaps Picasso didn't live in Málaga very long. You can learn about his childhood and his work at the Fundación Municipal Pablo Ruiz Picasso, but there is nothing about his later life in this museum.
  Picasso painted with different techniques and styles (this information is stated). He not only did oil paintings, but drawings, sculptures and ceramic works too.

9 *Your own answer. Possible answer:*
  I'd be interested in visiting both museums. I tried to see Guernica in Madrid, but the museum was closed the day I went (Tuesday).

B

1 *Your own answer. Possible answer*:
I know that Picasso was born in Málaga. That's all I know about him.

2 *Your own answer. Possible answer*:
The title *Picasso's return* suggests that Picasso left Málaga and returned there. The text might be about what happened when he returned. I'm not sure how this connects with a tourist brochure, however.

3 *Your own answer. Possible answer*:
I was completely wrong! The text is not about a return trip Picasso made to Málaga. The text says that Picasso left Málaga in 1901 and it does not say that he returned. In fact, the words 'If Picasso were to come back and visit the people of Málaga' suggest that he never came back. The text also aims to describe some of the most important tourist sites in Málaga.

4 The places mentioned are: Plaza de la Merced, Picasso Museo, park, Diputación Provincial, Calle Larios (street name), Plaza de la Constitución, Cathedral, Alcazaba, Palacio de La Aduana, Noble Hospital, Plaza de Toros, Castillo de Gibralfaro.
Your own answer. Possible answer:

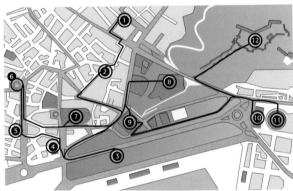

1 Fundación Municipal Pablo Ruiz Picasso	5 Calle Larios	9 Palacio de La Aduana
2 Picasso Museum	6 Plaza de la Constitución	10 Noble Hospital
3 Park	7 Cathedral and Museum	11 Plaza de Toros
4 Diputación Provincial	8 Alcazaba	12 Castillo de Gibralfaro

5 a Park, Plaza de la Constitución
   b Fundación Municipal Pablo Ruiz Picasso, Picasso Museum, Palacio de La Aduana, Noble Hospital
   c Plaza de la Merced, Calle Larios

6 *Your own answers. Possible answers*:
He left Málaga in January 1901, at the age of 19.
His paintings do not contain 'blazing images' of trees.
Paintings by his father and his teacher Muñoz Degrain are on display in a museum at the Government Office. This means that Picasso had painting lessons when he lived in Málaga.
He must have been to a bullfight if his first painting was of one.

Focus on the second conditional

1 b
2 a landed; would hear
   b ran/went; would see
   c visited; would enjoy
   d climbed/walked/went; would look
3 *Your own answer. Possible answer*:
If I were to go back and visit Florida, I would go to the Kennedy Space Centre. I have heard it's fantastic.

Unit6

Get ready to read

● c (above the puzzle it says *Yesterday's solutions* – you would see this in a newspaper but not in a book)
● 2

7	6	1	9	3	4	8	2	5
3	5	4	6	2	8	1	9	7
9	2	8	1	5	7	6	3	4
2	1	9	5	4	6	3	7	8
4	8	3	2	7	9	5	1	6
5	7	6	3	8	1	9	4	2
1	9	5	7	6	2	4	8	3
8	3	2	4	9	5	7	6	1
6	4	7	8	1	3	2	5	9

● *Your own answers.*

A

1 *Your own answer.*
2 b
3 a 4 b 1 c 3 d 2
4 Paragraph 1 contains three rhetorical questions. The first question – *Su who?* – is not a rhetorical question; it's something that people sometimes say to each other as a joke. (Sue, is short for Susan, is a girl's name.)
5 a

> The secret of its allure? <u>Su Doku is a game with very simple aims and rules, but limitless scope for complex ramifications and subtle strategies.</u> But perhaps its phenomenal success really only proves that, whether in Bangkok or Baldock, <u>people love to escape from the real world, with all its unresolvable dilemmas and random irritants, into a realm where reason rules supreme, and where every problem has a perfect solution</u> – even if the process of finding it leaves us frothing with frustration.

b

> <u>Su who? Was it only 20 months ago that this innocent quip first echoed around these offices? Only 600 days since *The Times* launched an unknown number puzzle on an unsuspecting public? Only 600 days since Wayne Gould's addictive grids began to nibble at our spare time, self-esteem, sang-froid, even our sanity?</u> It seems unbelievable. Chess took 600 years to spread across the medieval world. Other pastimes – Aussie-rules football, Eton fives, morris dancing – wouldn't catch on if you gave them 600 centuries.

Answer key

c

> And, as our correspondents report here, pick up any number of newspapers on five continents and you find half a billion puzzlers getting a daily dose of nine-by-nines. <u>Su Doku is huge in America and India – where Compulsive Su Doku syndrome is a recognised psychiatric complaint and beauty queens vie to complete puzzles on live TV. It appears in 60 Chinese papers and is a national craze in Japan, where a million people consider themselves *otaku*, or obsessives.</u>

d

> Yet in 600 days Su Doku has bewitched, bothered and bewildered populations across the globe. <u>Tap those two little words into Google and you get 90 million hits. Peruse any bookshop and you find dozens of Su Doku manuals,</u> some written as earnestly as philosophical tracts.

6 1 c (The author says that they would take 600 centuries, i.e. 60,000 years to become popular, whereas Su Doku is such a popular phenomenon that it has only taken 600 days.)

  2 b

  3 a (Baldock is in the south of England – it is a medium-sized town with a population of 10,000. Baldock's main supermarket, Tesco, is situated in a building that used to be a purpose-built film studio. By 1963 the building film studio had become the Kaysor Bondor Ballroom. On 21 December 1963, the Rolling Stones played at the ballroom. This is its main claim to fame!)

7 *Your own answer. Possible answer:*
I think he probably likes it but finds it frustrating. He says that it is a game with 'simple aims and rules' (paragraph 4) and 'every problem has a perfect solution' (paragraph 4). He also says that the 'addictive grids nibble at our spare time, self-esteem, sang-froid, even our sanity' (paragraph 1). In addition, when talking about the reasons why people are so keen on Su Doku, he says 'even if the process of finding it (the solution) leaves us frothing with frustration'. These things sound as if they could refer to the author himself.

B

1 *Your own answer. Possible answer:*
I think the article might be about someone who has become addicted to Sudoku.
2 When Robert Lipsyte tried Sudoku, his life changed – and not in a good way.
3 paragraph 7

Focus on the suffixes *-ful* and *-less*

1 mindful is possible but not 'forgetless'
2

		-ful	-less
a	limit		✓
b	care	✓	✓
c	wonder	✓	
d	home		✓
e	colour	✓	✓
f	stress	✓	

4 a paragraphs 1–7   b paragraphs 8–12
5 a He has been wasting energy over problems he couldn't solve, getting angry, jealous, wanting more.
  b His mind has been tired and forgetful.
  c He has been worrying about the war (the war in Iraq), the polar icecaps, airport insecurity.
  d He tried word puzzles.
  e He hated them.
  f Sudoku was truly mindless.
6 He loathed it.
7 a paragraph 9 (Meditation was much harder …) and paragraph 12 (If that thought …) describe events or facts
  b paragraph 11 (But I do think …) gives his opinions
  c paragraph 8 (I ditched Sudoku …) and paragraph 10 (I'm not feeling smug …) is about both
  d paragraph 11 (But I do think …) includes rhetorical questions. Robert Lipsyte uses these to give his opinions.
8 a Robert Lipsyte uses 'they' to refer to the 'psychologists, life coaches, social commentators' which he has mentioned in paragraph 2. It is the same 'they' each time.
  b He uses the expression 'weapons of mass distraction' because it is so close to 'weapons of mass destruction' – weapons that can kill thousands or millions of people over a large area. He has probably mentioned this deliberately to link up with the world issues he has just mentioned (war, poverty, the environment) and the issues of 'the war, the polar icecaps, airport insecurity' which he has mentioned twice.
  c Can you get more mindless than that? (paragraph 4)
9 a He used to waste energy chewing over problems he couldn't solve.
  b Now that he is doing meditation, he has learnt how not to waste energy.
10 *Your own answer. Possible answer:*
He found Sudoku mindless in a very negative sense. Sudoku takes up your time and allows you to put all your problems, both personal and political, to one side and to ignore them. It wasn't what he needed. Meditation instead has provided him with the means of dealing with the problems in his life.

He uses *mind games* in the title because he has used the words 'mindless' and 'mindful' a lot. Also, he feels that people are being manipulated into playing Su Doku as a distraction from more important issues that threaten our lives. He uses 'they' to refer to unseen people/forces to reflect the way in which mind games are sometimes played with prisoners to get them to talk. Most people don't agree, however, with the author's view!

Review 1

A 1 T 2 F 3 T 4 F 5 T 6 F
C 7 b 8 b
D 9 a 10 f 11 c 12 g 13 d
E 14 nuisance 15 effective 16 dusk 17 suspended
18 soothing
F 19 passengers who flew from Roissy to Toronto
20 Manager, Customer Relations
21 Toronto Airport 22 21st July 20__
23 technical problems
G 24 F 25 F 26 F 27 T 28 T 29 F 30 T

Unit 7

Get ready to read

○ a flowers b meat c T-shirts d cars
e chocolate
○ *Your own answers.*

A

1 A 3 B 2 C 5 D 1 E 4
2 a price b price
3 a Globale Fleischimport wanted to buy 2,500 kg in total. (They wanted to buy 500 kg for three of the weeks and 1,000 for one of the weeks.)
b They are going to get 500 kg for all four of the weeks, 2,000 kg in total.
c Globale Fleischimport wanted to pay USD 4,700 per ton.
d They are going to have to pay USD 4,900.
e Meat Corporation can only provide 500 kg each week. Meat Corporation wanted them to pay USD 5,000, and would not accept USD 4,700. Globale Fleischimport then accepted the slightly reduced price of USD 4,900 because they appreciate the good quality of Meat Corporation.
4 *See Exercise 5 for example questions.*
5 *Your own answers.*
6 2 f 3 b 4 d 5 a 6 c

Focus on missing words

1 1 a N b A
2 a N b A
2 accept (your) quote – C
quote (for the) following quantities – D
(the) production date – D
(the) best we can do – E

7 *Your own answers. Possible answers:*
production date, ton, fob, maximum, market, competitors
offer, produce, accept, appreciate
Please consider / reply / confirm
Thanks for prompt reply
Looking forward to hearing from you. / Best regards

B

1

	Email A	Email B
1 make an apology		
2 make an enquiry	✓	
3 make an urgent request		✓
4 make an offer		
5 give information	✓	✓

2 Email B is more direct because the writer is making an urgent request. (Fabio is at fault and the shipment is blocked, i.e. held up.)
3 She hopes that Ricardo (A) will be available on Monday August 3rd or Tuesday August 4th.
She hopes that Fabio (B) will act promptly and send the missing health certificate.
4 a some good news and some bad news (The good news is that he can meet them in August. The bad news is that he can't meet them on the suggested dates.)
b only good news
5

	Email C	Email D
1 make an apology	✓*	✓
2 make an enquiry		
3 make an urgent request		
4 make an offer	✓	
5 give information	✓	✓

*NB In email C, 'I'm afraid' could be considered an apology.

6 C
7 Tuesday 4th   pm: (will be) met at airport by Food Incorporated driver
(will) stay Sheraton Hotel (3 single rooms)

Wednesday 5th	(will be) picked up by Ricardo 9 am, visit of the plant and feedlot, dinner with Ricardo (will) stay Sheraton Hotel
Thursday 6th	Thursday early am: (will be) taken to airport by Food Incorporated driver

Unit8

Get ready to read
Your own answers.

A

1 You are probably pleased. You've got an interview!
2 *Your own answers. Possible answers:*
   You can arrive on time. You can be dressed smartly. You can look and sound confident and enthusiastic.
4 *Your own answers. Possible answers:*
   Paragraph 1: Arrival / Don't be late
   Paragraph 2: At reception
   Paragraph 3: Dress / Dress appropriately
   Paragraph 4: The interview begins
5 a N   b N   c N   d N
6 There are two topics. The topics are: non-verbal communication and verbal communication. Paragraphs 1 and 2 are about non-verbal communication, Paragraph 4 is about verbal communication, and Paragraph 3 links the two topics.
7

(1) Speak with authority and confidence, but never arrogance. (2) Be aware of your voice speed, volume and pitch – take deep breaths and be calm, measured and assured. Like any situation involving an element of negotiation, (3) don't attempt to speak first unless necessary, and (4) don't fill empty silences with meaningless words and phrases. Also, (5) try not to use filler phrases, e.g. 'You know what I mean' or 'I guess' – these phrases are ambiguous and lack conviction.

8 *Your own answer. Possible answer:*
   I hadn't really thought that what you did at reception might be important. Before my last interview, I just waited until someone came to collect me.

Focus on related words

word in texts	related words
arrive (v)	arrival (n)
sure (adj)	ensure (v)
reception (n)	receptionist (n)
communicate (v)	communication (n)
mean (v)	meaningless (adj)

B

1 You might be asked all these questions.
2 *Your own answers.*
3 Questions a and c are mentioned.
4 a 1, 2, 5   b 3, 7   c 4, 6
5 a
6 *Your own answers. Possible answers:*
   Yes, the advice seems good. The sentences in brackets explain why the interviewer is asking the question. If you can work out why the interviewer is asking a particular question, then you can adapt your answer in order to take into account the reason.
7 *Your own answers.*

Unit9

Get ready to read
○ *Your own answers.*
◉ a 3   b 2   c 1

A

1 a
2 a 4 b 6 c 5 d 1 e 3 f 2
3 19 (She will have worked ten complete months before March 31st, which means 19 days' holiday. She won't get any time off for the work she did in May – even though she worked for almost three-quarters (75%) of the month.)
4 *Your own answers. Possible answers:*
   a Two things can happen. Imagine you still have five days' holiday and you decide to leave the company on Friday December 8th. Either you can take your annual holiday before this date – even leaving on Friday December 1st. Alternatively, you can work until December 8th as you planned and you will get paid five extra days' wages when you leave.
   b If you don't take up to five days' holiday, then you may be able to have these days' holiday in the next financial year. However, you have to discuss this with your boss.
   c Yes, you get one extra day's holiday – a floating day – at Christmas. (A floating day is an official day's holiday that isn't fixed – you can take it when you like.)
   d If you have to work on a public holiday, you can take a day off another time.

B

1 *Cycle* in *Changes to pay cycle* refers to the main meaning SERIES. If people are paid on the last Thursday of the month, then the *pay cycle* refers to a series of events which happen in order, i.e. as they move from one month to the next, they are always paid on the last Thursday of the month.

2 a The letter is from Tina Grey, Group General Manager, Personnel Services.

  b It is to everyone who works at Jackson & Brown Ltd. (This is why Yoshima's address isn't in the top left-hand corner of the letter.)

3 a paragraph 1   d paragraph 2   g paragraph 3
  b paragraph 1   e paragraph 3   h paragraph 3
  c paragraph 2   f paragraph 3   i paragraph 4

4 a The changes are that the pay cycle will change from monthly to every four weeks.

  b The reason for this change is to enable Jackson & Brown Ltd to improve the efficiency of the payroll system and to make it easier for the staff to understand what they have been paid.

  c The changes will start on 13 September.

  d The cycle will continue with the payment of employees on 11 October, 8 November, 6 December, etc.

  e They might have problems with monthly pay routines, for example mortgage or rent payments.

  f They are offering a loan facility for a maximum of three weeks' pay.

  g Employees have to complete and return the form by 30 June if they want a loan.

  h The loan facility will be paid on 13 September.

  i If they wish to discuss the contents of the letter, their line manager will have further information. If they still have concerns or they have a personal query which they wish to discuss, they can call the following number: 01204 249259.

5 *Your own answer. Possible answer*:
I pay my rent and most of my bills every month, so I'd prefer the original pay cycle. I'd rather be paid every month than every four weeks.

Focus on compound nouns

1 Words in the text: *basic pay, pay day, pay routines, net pay, payslip*
2 a payroll b basic pay c pay day d payslip
   e net pay f pay routines
3 Compound nouns connected with work: pay agreement, pay award, pay cheque, pay claim, pay cut, pay deal, pay demand, pay dispute, pay freeze, pay increase, pay levels, pay negotiations, pay offer, pay rates, pay scale, pay structure

---

Unit 10

Get ready to read

Your own answers.

A

1 a The first problem that she mentions in her email is that she was late for work three times the previous week. The second problem is that she's got a dentist's appointment at 4.30 on Thursday afternoon. She will need to leave work early for this, but she hasn't asked her boss if she can do this.

  b *Your own answers. Possible answers*:
  She probably needs to leave home earlier in order to get to work by 8.30 am. I think she'd better mention the dentist's appointment to her boss as soon as she can. If she needs to leave the office at 4 o'clock, she should tell her boss that she will either work during her lunch hour or she will work an extra hour the following day. Alternatively, she could have two 30-minute lunch breaks on two days.

2 *Your own answer. Possible answer*:
Flexitime is a system of working in which people *have to be at work for certain fixed periods of time, but they can choose when to start or finish work.*

3 flexible (working hours) 1, 2
  flexible (lunch hour) 2
  (has the) flexibility (to clock in/out) 2
  (One of the best-liked features of flexitime is) flexileave

4 a The other words connected with banking are: owe, accounting period, credit, debit, go into debt.

  b The similarity is that the debit margin is like an overdraft – you can spend more money than you have, but only up to your debit limit. The difference is that being in credit in the bank is a very good thing – and there is no 'surplus beyond your credit margin'.

5 1 She was late for work three times last week because of the rush-hour traffic.
  2 She has to go to the dentist on Thursday afternoon.

What are the advantages for employees?
- Allows you to schedule your travel time to avoid congestion (1)
- Allows you bank time to be used for leisure/personal activities (2)
- Personal matters can be sorted without having to take time off (2)
- Parents can schedule their day to pick up young children
- Reduces absenteeism (2)
- Reduces stress and fatigue and unfocused employees
- Increases morale
- Increases employee satisfaction and production

6

What are the advantages for employers?
- A benefit to retain and attract new employees
- Work time visits to doctor/dentist are in employee's time (2)
- Measures employee's attendance – you only pay for time in attendance. Late arrival caused by traffic congestion, delayed trains, etc. is at employee's expense (1)
- An incentive to complete tasks instead of being carried forward to the next day as extra hours worked count towards the final target

7 c

8 *Your own answers. Possible answers* :

Many people might always take the same day off, especially Friday, and there would not be enough people to keep the office running.

The employer would have to keep a check on how many hours the staff were working, which would be an additional responsibility for him/her.

9 *Your own answer. Possible answer:*

The main reason I'd like to work flexitime is that you could have a morning/afternoon or a whole day off every month.

Focus on phrasal verbs

1 a start b lose c collect

2 b fix up c given up d do up e split up
  f brought up

B

1 *Your own answers. Possible answers:*

a People will not take time off work when they need to go to the dentist, etc. Flexible working hours will allow these personal activities within the working day. No one should ever be late again!

b All the staff will only be in the office at certain periods of the day. Meetings will have to be arranged within these fixed/core hours. In addition, incoming phone calls during the flexitime periods may be missed.

c Either employees will keep their own records of working hours – the boss will have to trust them. Or, and more likely, there will have to be a system of recording how many hours people work.

d It is unlikely to be abused if it is monitored properly.

2 c

3 All the sentences are false. The style and language is quite different from the webpage in Reading A. In Reading B, the webpage is written in an impersonal style – the word *you* doesn't appear once, for example. In addition, there are lots of long words, especially nouns. In the first sentence, for example, nine of the words have ten or more letters!

4 a systems b information c records d queries
  e system

5 a management information

b attendance data

c web browser

d employee absence history

e employee attendance record

password clearance

staff attendance

staffing information

desktop PCs

attendance reports

attendance record(s)

attendance details

user ID

---

6 *Your own answer. Possible answer:*

Information is recorded on a database and is then available on an Intranet website. You need password clearance to browse the website.

7 *Your own answer. Possible answer:*

This shows how working hours and credits/debits are recorded.

8 *Your own answer. Possible answer:*

ATRACS is a package you can buy for staff to record their attendance. With such a system in place, we'd be able to implement flexitime here. It shows how many hours each person is in credit or debit, so you can make sure that people are working the correct number of hours. We can have a demonstration if you're interested.

9 *Your own answer. Possible answer:*

I think having a half-day or a day off is great. However, I work for a fairly small company and we all work quite hard. We get on well with the owner, and he's OK about requests for time off.

Unit 11

○ a memo b report c agenda d minutes

○ *Your own answers.*

A

1 a

2 No, she didn't attend. (Her name appears under *Apologies* at the end of the meeting – this means that she has apologised for her absence from the meeting.)

3 yes (The issue is 'Removal of study grants'. It was raised by someone else.)

4 b

5 *Your own answer. Possible answer:*

Yes, I think we would discuss the same type of things if we had this kind of meeting. However, I work for a small company, so we just talk directly to our boss and colleagues. We don't have any meetings.

Focus on reported speech

1 *The council asked* if it would be possible to have the phone system changed so that international calls can be made.

The council enquired if the correct route for raising recycling issues was through John Evans, Office Services Manager.

The council requested that a healthy range of snacks be available from the snack machine.

The council asked for clarification of the expenses policy.

2 b Is the correct route for raising recycling issues through John Evans, Office Services Manager?

c Could a healthy range of snacks be available from the snack machine?

d Can you clarify the expenses policy?

B

1 Alejandro Mendoza
2 *Your own answers. Possible answers*:
Where will the classes take place?
How long will the course last?
3 *See Exercise 4 for the answers.*
4 a COURSE MATERIAL
  b TIMING AND LOCATION
  c TEACHER
  d ENROLMENT
  e COURSE CONTENT / COURSE MATERIAL
  f LEVEL
  g No costs are mentioned. Esteban would like some preparation time and some time off in lieu for his teaching time, but no payments are mentioned at all.
5 a You might have to buy a book – or the company could buy a class set.
  b There will be two lessons a week, of an hour each.
  c No, Alejandro won't teach you. Esteban will be the teacher.
  d Anyone can enrol, but the course is aimed at people who use Spanish in their jobs.
  e You will study how to deal with Spanish-speaking visitors, and how to deal with telephone and email queries.
  f No, you don't need to know any Spanish in order to do the course. The level of the course is elementary and students will be either beginners or know only a little Spanish.
  g No costs are mentioned, but it probably won't cost anything. You might have to buy the book.
6 5 6 7 (The Personnel Manager might need to discuss the following issues with the Managing Director: (5) the timing of the course – whether or not it takes place in work time; (6) the cost of books – whether or not the company pays; (7) whether Esteban can have preparation time built into his working hours and time off in lieu if the lessons were to be given at lunchtime. These are important issues which she cannot resolve.)
7 *Your own answer. Possible answer*:
I think the students should buy the books so that they can keep them and refer to them outside the lesson. I'd be happy if the company bought the books, but I think the students should be able to keep them. Also, I think the ideas are very nice, but I hope Esteban doesn't have to work too hard.
8 *Your own answer. Possible answer*:
My language is Hungarian and I have never taught it. I don't know if there are any books available. I hope I have learnt something about teaching from my own English classes.
9 *Your own answer. Possible answer*:
I have never done an in-house course, but my sister did a course in English before she went to a conference in Los Angeles. It wasn't in her office, but she was in a small group with three of her colleagues so I think it counts as in-house. They went to Lake Balaton for a week and did a very intensive course – just the four of them. My sister said it was very useful.

Unit 12

Get ready to read
Your own answers.

A

1 GETTING ORGANISED (option a) is the first section in the book. You must get organised before you go to an overseas university. You will only begin your studies (option b) and your university life (option c) when you get there.
2 (1) but
  (2) In addition
3 a Reputation
  b Entry requirements
  c The country
  d Available places
4 *Your own answers. Possible answers*:
the cost, the length of the course, how many other students from your country there are
5 *Your own answers. Possible answers*:
  a Furthermore, their students are often brilliant at their subject.
  a However, this does not mean that they are the best place for you.
  b For example, you need lower grades to study engineering than to study medicine.
  b Therefore, make sure you check your grades before you try to enrol.
  c (Maybe a family member has studied there) and told you what it's like.
  c (Maybe a family member has studied there) or you've been there on holiday.
  d (Sometimes it is very difficult to get a place on a particular course, such as Law,) even though you've got good grades.
  d (Sometimes it is very difficult to get a place on a particular course, such as Law,) since it is a very popular subject.
7 *Your own answer. Possible answer*:
I think Meeting students from your country and The university site are the least important reasons. All the others are very important, in my view.

B

1 The best place for Akihiro to start is probably www.iefa.com. He isn't already living in the United States (therefore, not www.isoa.org). Also, it's better to start with a free website than to have to pay (as in www.globalgrant.com).
2 *Your own answer. Possible answer*:
When I think of Australia, I think of the Great Barrier Reef, Sydney Harbour Bridge and sport.
4 *Your own answer. Possible answer*:
I think the homepage will say that Australia has lots to offer the international student – modern universities, excellent teaching, international feel, for example. The aim of this homepage is to 'sell' Australia.

5 *Your own answers. Possible answers*:

Growing Destination – Australia is becoming more popular as a destination for students.

Global Recognition – Australian universities are becoming better known.

Cost of Living – Australia is not as expensive as some countries.

Diversity – you can study lots of different subjects in Australia.

Technology – Australian universities have all the latest technology.

Work – there is lots of work available for you after you have studied in Australia.

6 *Your own answers. Possible answers*:

a a centre of learning.

b recognized throughout the world.

c less than you might think.

d a wide range of different subjects.

e the education system is the best in the world.

f you to work while you are a student.

8 *Your own answer. Possible answer*:

I'd love to study there. The only problem for me is that it is a long, long way from home (Hungary).

Focus on *this* and *these*

1 a wide open spaces of outback bush, kangaroos, koalas and clean air and water

b the cost of living and tuition fees in Australia (which) are much lower than compared to the USA or the UK

c the chance to work up to 20 hours per week during term time, and during vacations (to) work full time

2 a Australia is in the top ten spenders in the world for Research and Development and 2% of all scientific papers come from Australia

b (the fact that) Australia is in the top ten spenders in the world for Research and Development and 2% of all scientific papers come from Australia

---

Unit 13

Get ready to read

● *Your own answers.*

A

1 b

2 The passage mentions topics a and c. The first paragraph and the first sentence of the second paragraph are about topic c, and the rest of the passage is about topic a.

3 a T b F c T d T e T f F g T h F i F

4

Obstacles to faster effective reading

Perhaps you have seen very young children – or older people – learning to read. They move the index finger along the line of print, pointing to each word, sometimes even to individual letters, saying the word or letters to themselves in a low voice. (a) This is called 'vocalizing'. Sometimes the learner makes no sound though his lips may move to form the words, sometimes there is not even any perceptible movement of the mouth at all, but the learner is still activating his throat muscles slightly to 'say' the words to himself. He is still vocalizing.

However slight the extent of vocalizing may be it will still be impossible for such a reader to reach a speed of more than 280 w.p.m. (b) The appreciation of written words must be entirely visual and we must read more than one word at a time.

Look at 'you', the second word of this passage. Even if you look straight at the 'o' of that word, without moving your eyes at all you can clearly see 'perhaps' and 'have' on either side. (c) So you can read three words at once. Now look at the word 'word' on line 2. With a very slight movement of the eyes, you can take in the whole phrase '… saying the word or letters …' in the same glance. In the same way, you can probably take in a complete short sentence on one line, like the one on line 3, at one glance. None of the lines of print on a page this size should need more than four or five eye movements. Take line 4. This would perhaps break up into four word groups: (1) … may move to form the words … (2) … sometimes there is not even … (3) … any perceptible movement … (4) … of the mouth at all, but the … When you are reading well, your eyes will be one or two word groups ahead of the one your mind is taking in. (d)

Practise on something easy and interesting

Many students trying to increase their effective reading speed become discouraged when they find that if they try to race through a passage faster, they fail to take in what they have read. (e) The problem here is that the material they are practising on is either too difficult for them in vocabulary or content, (f) or not sufficiently interesting. Read things you like reading. (g) Go to the subject catalogue in the library. Biography, sport, the cinema … there is bound to be some area that interests you and in which you can find books of about your level of ability or just below.

If you want a quick check on how easy a book is, read through three or four pages at random. If there are, on average, more than five or six words on each page that are completely new to you, then the book is not suitable for reading-speed improvement. (h/i)

5 Information is given for the first three statements in *Get ready to read*. The statements are all false.

B

1 *Your own answers. Possible answers*:

a Try not to let your eyes regress.

b Don't vocalize.

c Read words in groups.

d Practise speed reading on material that is not too difficult.

2 There are three hints. Think of the passage as a whole; Pay attention to paragraph structure; Dictionaries slow you down!

3 1 b 2 a 3 c 4 c 5 a 6 c

4 *Your own answers. Possible answers*:

a For speed reading practice, a dictionary is unnecessary.

b If you really want to know what all the words mean, make a note and check later.

c Even if you don't know a word, you can often get the meaning by working it out from context.

5 a

6 *Your own answers. Possible answers*:

2 The importance of both the topic sentence in a paragraph, and the first and last paragraphs in a text.

3 The use of context in working out the meaning of unknown words.

7 Information is given for the last three statements in *Get ready to read*. The statements are all false.

Focus on words in context

a 4 b 5 c 6 d 3 e 2 f 1 g 9 h 10
i 7 j 8

Unit 14

Get ready to read

● These four books are all reference books. Other reference books include: dictionary, almanac, encyclopaedia. Also: books like *The Guinness Book of Records*, and many other non-fiction books.
● a 4 b 3 c 6 d 5 e 2 f 1
● *Your own answer.*

A

1 *Your own answers. Possible answers*:
Do all Americans work long hours, or only certain types of workers?
If people work long hours, why do they do this?
2 d *Contemporary America* is the most useful because it is about America today.
a This is a travel guide.
b This is about the history of the United States.
c This book is about President J. F. Kennedy's mother, sisters and wife.
3 *Your own answer.*
4 society, politics, economy, culture, and world role of the United States
5 yes – Society, The Political System, The Economy, Culture, Foreign Policy
6 a Chapter 8 The Economy – perhaps one of the first three sections – looks as if it might be the most useful.
b No chapter heading mentions the specific word *work*.
7 a no
b working hours
8 yes – (220–1) Chapter 8 The Economy

B

1

Laws prevent employers from discriminating in hiring on the basis of age, sex, race, religion, physical handicaps or national origin. There are laws to maintain safe working conditions and to allow release time for childbirth, adoption, or to care for sick relatives. The United States has had a federally-mandated work week and minimum wage since 1938, when the maximum hours an individual can be required to work was set at 40 hours and the base wages put at $0.25 an hour. In 2005, all full-time workers over 18 years old were guaranteed at least $5.15 an hour; those under 18, or those in jobs where tips made up a large part of their salaries might receive less. At minimum wage, a full-time (40-hours-a-week) worker would make $206 a week before taxes. Moreover, 12 states have laws putting minimum wages above the national requirement. Washington sets it at $7.16, Connecticut at $7.10, and California at $6.75, for example (DOL, 2005). Most businesses pay higher wages than are required by law, usually about $7 an hour for beginners. In 2000, the average hourly pay for all US wage and salaried workers was $16.17 an hour (AP, 2001d). Any work done beyond the 40-hour maximum is subject to overtime pay at a higher rate of 1.5 to 2 times the hourly rate. In 2004, the average worker took home three hours of overtime pay per week.

2 The information answers question b – the maximum hours an individual can work is 40 hours.

3

One in three American workers say that they are "overwhelmed" with the amount of work required of them (Joyner, 2001). With technological advances speeding up assembly lines, companies have "downsized" the number of workers while asking them to increase output by working faster and longer. Part of the problem has been that with personal consumption – with high home mortgages and transportation costs – and the fears of an economic slowdown male workers work harder to prove their worth. Those who work long hours hope to be among those retained if and when downsizing comes. Of course, this is a numbers game as two in three workers do not feel overwhelmed, say that they are satisfied with their jobs, and do not fear layoffs (Harris Poll, 2000d). Beyond the office, technology is affecting hours as e-mail, voice recorders, and cellphones allow the job to spill over into home life. Additionally, the average two-way commute nationwide adds 48 minutes to the workday. For those working in big cities like New York and living in the suburbs, commutes can often total 1.5 hours each way.

5 No – it is about mobility in the workforce
6 Conclusion
7 *Your own answer. Possible answer*:
I got the impression from the text on page 221 that a lot of people worked more than 40 hours a week.
8 *Your own answer. Possible answer*:
No, it doesn't surprise me. Americans work 9 weeks more than people in Europe, so they must have shorter holidays in order to do this.
9 *Your own answer. Possible answer*:
maximum working hours = 40 per week by law (since 1938); however Americans work about 350 hours (9 weeks) more than workers in Europe

Focus on US English

1 workforce; holiday
2 a high-school – secondary (GB English)
   b stayed home – stayed at home (GB English)
   c licenses – licences (GB English)
   d paychecks – pay cheques (GB English)
   e neighborhoods – neighbourhoods (GB English, although *areas* would be more common in GB English)
3 5 Society

Unit 15

Get ready to read

⊙ a 800,000 b Seventy c Forty d One
  e 1,700 f Four g three (proceed, exceed, succeed)
  h 600

A

1 no
2 An iceberg is a very large mass of ice which floats in the sea. About 90% of an iceberg is submerged, which means that only a small part – or its tip – is visible. When we say that something is 'the tip of the iceberg', we mean that this is a small noticeable part of the problem. Here, 'a few statistics' are the tip of the iceberg (not a problem, in this case), but we don't know about the much greater numbers of people who are 'hidden'.
3 Most people who are using this book are probably students of English as a foreign language.
4 speakers of English as a second language

> The second part of the language-learning iceberg relates to people who live in countries where English has no official status, but where it is learned as a foreign language in schools and institutes of higher education, and through the use of a wide range of 'self-help' materials.

5 The best summary is probably a. (The paragraph doesn't say anything about an increase in the number of people learning English (b). Summary c is a paraphrase (a repetition in different words in a simpler or shorter form which makes the original clearer) of the sentence *There are only hints as to what the numbers involved might be*. This sentence is part of the main point of the paragraph, but it is not all of it.)
6 a
7 In paragraph 2, *total* appears in the last sentence and in the first sentence in paragraph 3.
In paragraph 3, *China* appears in the last sentence and in the first sentence in paragraph 4.
In paragraph 4, *successful* appears in the last sentence and in the first sentence in paragraph 5.

8 b: The main point is the difficulty of finding out how many people speak English as a foreign language (as in previous paragraph, and part of the introduction).
9 paragraph 3: The main point and topic sentence is *In China, there has been an explosion of interest in the English language in recent years.*
paragraph 4: The topic is English as the dominant language of world communication. The topic sentence is: *There is enormous motivation (to be successful in achieving fluency in English), given the way that English has become the dominant language of world communication.*
10 paragraph 2 1 example – China.
paragraph 3 2 examples – 1) *Follow Me*, 2) new programmes for scientific and business users
paragraph 4 7 general examples – 1) books, etc. 2) air travel, 3) maritime language, 4) international business, academic conferences, diplomacy, sport, 5) scientific writing, 6) mail, 7) computers
Three specific examples – 1) Japanese company, 2) Colombian doctor, 3) Danish student
11 *Your own answer. Possible answer*:
Students who go to Spain or Latin America to do a Spanish course find that English is the main language for communication outside the classes.

B

1 a

Focus on participle adjectives

1 developing, developed
2 a stolen b sleeping c disappointing
   d surprising e proposed f rented

2 a The topic is the use of English words all over the world.
   b The topic sentence is: *… The 'Americanization' of world culture … has caused English words to appear prominently in city streets all over the world …*
   c Six general examples – 1) popular songs / pop music, 2) films, 3) television, 4) high finance, 5) food and drink, 6) consumer goods
   Two specific examples – 1) foreign groups recording in English, 2) Brazilian child
3 *Your own answers. Possible answers*:
   a Lots of these words – especially words connected with culture, entertainment and consumer society – are used in Spanish. I have only come across the words *marketing* and *top secret*, however, from the words connected with politics and commerce and *boy scout* and *gangster* from the words connected with people and behaviour.

b   The words *cover girl*, *mob* and *pin up* are used in Spain. We also use the word *confidential*.

c   Here is the list of words from *The English language* for the category sport and tourism/transport, etc:
Sport: baseball, bobsleigh, clinch, comeback, deuce, football, goalie, jockey, offside, photo-finish, semi-final, volley, walkover
Tourism, transport etc.: antifreeze, camping, hijack, hitch-hike, jeep, joy-ride, motel, parking, picnic, runway, scooter, sightseeing, stewardess, stop (sign), tanker, taxi

4   Paragraph 2:
a   The topic is the non-approval of English loan words.
b   The topic sentence is *People who do not approve of American values or who are disturbed by rapidity of change are often strongly critical of the impact of English on their language – especially when an English word supplants a traditional word.*
c   Three examples – 1) *planta* in Spanish, 2) *mistletoe* in Dutch, 3) law in France, 4) laws in Brazil and Germany
Paragraph 3:
a   The topic is the approval of English loan words.
b   The topic sentence is *In particular, commercial firms and advertisers are well aware of the potential selling power that the use of English vocabulary can bring.*
c   Two examples – 1) several reports of an increase in sales, 2) Japanese television commercials
One non-commercial example – Dutch youth club
Paragraph 4:
a   The topic is the effect of English on word order in foreign languages.
b   The topic sentence is … *surveys are slowly bringing to light several cases where word order or word structure has been affected.*
c   Four examples – 1) active construction in Danish, 2) plural endings of loan words retained in foreign languages, 3) indefinite article in Swedish, 4) English word endings in Danish

5   *Your own answers. Possible answers*:
paragraph 2 – In Spain, we use the word *fabrica* for factory. Perhaps they use *planta* more in South America. I think the most international word of all is *football*. Today Spanish people always say *fútbol* instead of *balón pie*.
paragraph 3 – Most advertisements on Spanish TV are in Spanish, including Nike advertisements. Their slogan *Just do it* is always in English, however.
paragraph 4 – English plurals are now used as part of the Spanish language.

6   *Your own answers. Possible answers*:
paragraph 2 – I don't think laws against the use of English are a good idea. Nowadays there is greater movement of people – and there should be greater exchange of language.
paragraph 3 – Today marketing monopolises language and I am not in favour of this.

paragraph 4 – I think new vocabulary and modified word order/structure is natural evolution. Language is constantly changing.

7   *Your own answer. Possible answer*:
You would probably include these two topics – English as the language of world communication, the use of loan words in your language – but include your own examples.

Unit 16

Get ready to read
○   *Your own answers.*
○   Reading / Listening

A

1   2
2   5   £10 million   6   failures/crashes   7   large
8   banking (systems)   9   disastrous   10   programme
11   finding ways to stop   12   are untestable
13   critical networks   14   says
3   15   E   16   A   17   G   18   D
19   some systems are now so large they are untestable
scheme has been given added urgency
if a century-old technology like a power grid can fail

Focus on paraphrasing
b   H – the importance of our exam results
c   F – to repair my bike   d   I – get funding
e   C – always a measure of their quality   f   B – to build

B

2   1   £3.6bn   2   100 countries   3   Asia   4   American
5   a third   6   well-known   7   media   8   new
9   purchasing   10   outdated   11   temporary
12   novelty   13   overall
3   *Your own answer. Possible answer*:
I would like some further practice. I would also like to see examples of the other exam tasks.

Review 2

A   **1** T   **2** T   **3** F   **4** T   **5** T   **6** F   **7** F   **8** F
9 F   **10** T
C   **11** B   **12** D   **13** A   **14** C
D   **15** Y   **16** N   **17** Y   **18** Y
E   **19** F   **20** T   **21** T   **22** F
F   **23** once every two or three weeks
24 on the first day of class
25 talking
26 because only two or three people speak/not everyone talks
G   **27** b   **28** f   **29** h   **30** c

H 31 a

I 32 a **33** a **34** b **35** c **36** c

J *Your own answers. Possible answers*:

   37 If you cannot

   38 When you return

   39 If you are sick

   40 we may ask you to

   41 When you are off sick

   42 according to

K *Your own answers. Possible answers*:

   43 If you need to go to the dentist's, you should try and go in your own time.

   44 If you have to have an appointment during the working day, try and get one at the start or end of your shift.

   45 If you have lots of hospital appointments, you might need to take the time off as holiday.

L 46 c

M 47 and **48** a 2 d 3

N 49 3 **50** 2 **51** 2 **52** 3

0 53 sentence 3

   54 sentence 1

   55 sentence 2

P 56 sentence 1

Q 57 and **58** a, d

R 59 b

S 60 3